T0119443

Before I Go

Letters to Our Children about What Really Matters

Peter Kreeft

SHEED & WARD

Lanham • Chicago • New York • Toronto • Plymouth, UK

Published by Sheed & Ward
An imprint of Rowman & Littlefield Publishers, Inc.
4501 Forbes Boulevard, Suite 200
Lanham, MD 20706

Estover Road
Plymouth PL6 7PY
United Kingdom

Distributed by National Book Network

Library of Congress Cataloging-in-Publication Data

Kreeft, Peter.
  Before I go : letters to our children about what really matters / Peter Kreeft.
      p. cm.
  ISBN-13: 978-1-58051-224-4 (cloth : alk. paper)
  ISBN-10: 1-58051-224-0 (cloth : alk. paper)
   1. Conduct of life. 2. Christian life—Catholic authors. I. Title.

BJ1581.2.K73 2007
170'.44—dc22   2007019267

Printed in the United States of America.

♾™ The paper used in this publication meets the minimum requirements of American National Standard for Information Sciences—Permanence of Paper for Printed Library Materials, ANSI/NISO Z39.48-1992.

Introduction

My unutterably dear children (and grandchildren),

I give you this book about the most valuable life lessons I have learned because I want to give you everything I can, and writing books is something I can do. I wish I had given you more of myself, that I had been a stronger, wiser, and more present father to you. This book is a poor substitute for that. But its motive is not poor; its motive is my love for you, which is stronger than my love of life itself.

I wish I had shaped that love into stronger forms. Any parent, if only he or she is honest, humble, and loving, must regret not having had godlike powers to fulfill the godlike responsibility of being a God–stand-in, a parent. What a job! All the other jobs in the world combined can't compare.

Jesus didn't have to write any books because He lived all His teaching perfectly. No one else ever did. That's why we write books for each other. All books say, "Do as I say, not as I do." Even the Bible was written by sinners.

Love can take many forms. Let my love for you now take the form of this book. True, it is not an adequate substitute for the living words of a person, any more than banging on a drum is a substitute for being a drummer. Yet Jesus accepted the little drummer boy's gift, so please accept mine, in the same spirit, as a gift of love.

The order of these life lessons is random, deliberately undeliberate. They come in the order in which they were written, like life itself.

1. From the Dying to the Living

This book originated in my musing on Doctor Samuel Johnson's famous observation, "I know of no thought that so wonderfully concentrates a man's* mind as the thought that he will be hanged tomorrow morning."

As I begin this book I am still young (in my sixties) and in good health. It is hard to imagine that one day the hand that penned this will be the hand of a skeleton. But I know it is true. Death is life's one certain prognosis.

---

*Grammar note: As in all the prefeminist books, "man" here means males and females equally. I do not believe men are superior to women, but I do believe that inclusive language is superior to exclusive language. So I use "he" and "man" to mean males and females equally. What feminists call "inclusive language" is really exclusive language, and what they call "exclusive language" is really inclusive. Naturally, the sixties radicals who hated and killed femininity called themselves "feminists." And Mao Zedong's China was called "the people's republic."

C. S. Lewis says somewhere that no one should be allowed to die without having read Plato's *Symposium*. (I'd say his "Apology.") I think that I should not be allowed to die before saying these things to you. I have written dozens of books, and thousands of strangers have read them; it is high time I wrote one for four of the five people I love the most—my own children.

Nearly as universal as death is a parent's love for his children. But when the parent is dead, it's too late to share the most precious things he knows. The parent, thus, is in a dilemma: after he is dead, he can no longer speak; but before he dies, his words do not carry the weight of death with them, and they are lost in the crowd of other words. A dying man's words step up and come forth out of the crowd of other words, and they have an edge because their speaker stands at the edge. No child forgets the last words of a dying parent or vice versa. My father's last words to me were simply "I love you" and my last words to him were the same, and then "Go, Dad, under the mercy." Writing a book is a way of escaping that dilemma, for a book is like a ghost—it remains, even though it is not the living author but only his "remains." It is a word-insurance policy. It is a way of speaking even after you are dead.

These words are for *you*. Whether anyone else reads them is not my main concern. I have published this book only to give them the chance to overhear our conversation.

But this book is universal enough for all. I did not include the unique, the private things: John's giraffe Girard, Jenny's Raggedy Ann, Katherine's dead squirrel, and Bean's falling-apart, blue Binkie—or their psychological equivalents. Those are yours alone, part of the secret identity known only to you, your two procreators, and your Creator and Designer. (We all wear Designer genes.)

2. Who Am I To Give Advice?

Who am I to give advice to others; I, who need to take advice myself? Isn't this hypocritical?

No, it is not hypocritical, because I begin right here with the one thing I know we all need—absolute honesty. My advice is to admit that you need advice. Honesty and humility are almost the same thing.

But who am I to speak of *this*? Am I some kind of expert in humility? Can I be proud of my humility? Far from it. But if we were forbidden to preach or to hear preaching until we practiced, we would all be deaf and dumb.

Who am I to give advice? I'm like you.

3. The Best Thing in Life

My dear children, because I love you the most, I want to give you the best things in life. But I can't give you the very best thing because that is not a *thing* at all, and it is not something any of us can give to another. Each of us has to get it for himself or herself. I didn't get it from my parents, though they helped me enormously, and you can't get it from me, though I can try to help—and this book is part of that attempt.

What is the very best thing in life? The greatest good?

Everything in life is good for *something*. But maybe something is good for *everything*. The very best thing is. Everybody knows that there's something good in everything, but not everyone knows that there's everything good in something. One word for that something is "God." God is total, infinite goodness. If that isn't true, God isn't God and let's be atheists.

But how do you get this "best thing in life"? How do you "get" God? What can it mean to "have" Him?

Of course we can't "get" Him or possess Him. We can't even possess other human beings, though fools keep trying to. But we can *know* God and not just know *about* Him. We can be His friends. We can even spiritually marry Him! We can make Him in our lives what He is in fact: number one.

It's very simple: He's actually there, and we actually meet Him when we pray, whether we feel that or not, and He actually *does stuff to us* when we pray, whether we feel it or not. And that relationship is called "religion" (the word "religion" means, literally, "relationship"), and that is the very best thing we can do in this life because it's what we're going to be doing forever, and it's the only thing there is that's going to give us joy without boredom forever.

Everybody in the world knows that. We can all sense something like that, deep down. Christians know more: that since we couldn't make it up to Him, He came down to us and became one of us. He let down His "Jacob's ladder" from Heaven, and that ladder is not a thing but a person, with a face and a name and a place. And we can find that person, that face, that name, and that place very easily: just look at a crucifix. It's the world's most important road map.

4. If There Was Time to Say Just One Thing

If I knew there was only one minute left for us to talk to each other and after that minute we would never again see each other in this world, what would be the one thing I would most want to say to you and to hear you say to me?

"I love you," of course. But also, "I forgive you." Because love has enemies, and forgiveness destroys all those enemies.

Jesus thought forgiveness is so important that He made our salvation depend on it. He made us pray, "God, forgive us our wrongs *just as much as* we forgive those who have wronged us."

So I ask your forgiveness for neglecting you, misunderstanding you, not trying harder, not taking more responsibility for your lives, and not sharing with you more of my feelings, dreams, and wisdom (whatever that may be). Despite all that, I have always loved you, I always will, and I know you know that. I also know you love me and forgive me for all my faults. I know you accept my forgiveness for

9

all the little stupid things you've done. (Welcome to the human race.)

You've really been wonderful, lovable, beautiful kids. You gave us far, far less trouble and much more love than most kids do today. You deserve to be loved more than you are, and that's one of the reasons I'm glad there's a God—because He can do that even when I can't.

5. Everything Is Love

Not only is love everything, but everything is love.

Love is everything. Love is the soul of everything valuable. The most precious gift in the world given without love is worthless; the cheapest gift in the world given with love is priceless.

But everything is also love. Everything valuable is *made of* love. Everything that exists, from yourself to a grain of sand, is God's love made visible, made incarnate—love in the form of creation. The words He spoke to create everything in the universe—"let it be"—were the words of love. He loved stuff into being. Space is love's spread. The room you are in now is a thousand cubic feet of God's love spread out. Time is love's life ("lifetime"). History is love's drama. Matter is love's body. Gravity is love's energy when it moves not souls but stars and stones and storms. We are love's children. "Be made" means "I love you." Your very existence is God's love of you. Love is the meaning of life and the meaning of religion and the meaning of everything.

6. The Most Important Person

One of the stupidest songs I ever heard on TV was the theme song of a kids' show of the seventies, "The Electric Company." It said: "The most important person in the whole wide world is—you!" Implied message: be a self-centered little spoiled brat. You're number one, everyone else is number two.

Here is an alternative philosophy:

1. The most important person is God. This is as necessarily true as $2 + 2 = 4$. It is true whether you know it or not, whether you like it or not, whether you believe it or not. So you'd better learn to know it and like it and believe it.
2. The second most important person in the world is the person you marry. Nobody else comes even close. That's what marriage *is*. If you don't know that, you're not really married.
3. Next come your kids.

4. Then comes yourself. Take care of yourself before taking care of anyone else except your kids, your spouse, and your God. Because if you don't inflate your own oxygen mask first, you won't be able to help others inflate theirs.

5. Then comes your friends. Never betray a friend.

6. Then comes everyone else you know, your "neighbors."

7. Then comes the rest of the world.

8. Then comes things, any and all things: money, the things money can buy—houses, cars, and vacations. *Stuff.* (Remember George Carlin's routine about "stuff.") Always, people before things. Use things and love people, not vice versa.

9. Finally, abstractions: ideas, causes, organizations, political parties, etc. They are means to the rest as ends. By the way, the Church is not an "organization," it's a family. I never saw "organized religion," only disorganized religion, like Noah's ark.

7. Memento mori

That's Latin for "remember death." It's a medieval saying, and it's a good test of our perspective. Death (our own death) puts life into proper perspective. Things that seemed important recede into triviality when you're dying—things like fame and money and *stuff*. And things we usually ignore—things like love, trust, honesty, self-giving, and forgiveness—these stand out as infinitely more important in light of death. Death's dark light is pretty bright!

Whatever you can't take with you is only placenta, afterbirth. What you *can* take with you is the baby.

When Elizabeth was (mis-)diagnosed with a fatal brain tumor, I was amazed at how unimportant a thousand things suddenly became: paying bills, getting things done on schedule, and keeping up life's appearances, facades, makeup, all its sandcastles. They could all wait. One day soon it will all have to wait forever.

Ask yourself: what can't you take with you? And whatever answers you find, stop worrying about them now.

Ask yourself: what can you, will you, and must you take with you? And whatever answers you find, care about those things now.

"In the evening of our lives, we will be judged on our love." (St. John of the Cross)

The number one regret people have when dying is not having told their children or their parents how much they loved them.

The most destructive mistake in life is not forgiving, since forgiving is love's first deed.

What will be important to you on your deathbed? Let that be important to you now. Because you are on your deathbed now. As soon as you are born, you are born onto a deathbed. Nobody gets out of this place alive. Doctor Johnson is right: the thought of your death "wonderfully clarifies the mind." Demand clarity *now*.

8. A One-Minute, Life-Changing Prayer

I don't think the length of prayer is very important, but I know that the *habit* of praying many short prayers is. St. Paul says, "pray without ceasing." The power is in the not-ceasing. The two most important things about praying are the beginning and the not-ceasing. The rest is just detail.

What is your first thought each morning when you wake up to another day of life, another divine gift? That day did not come from yesterday. One day does not have the power to create another. God alone can create more time. Each day, each moment of time, comes straight from Him, from His act of creation, which is present, not just past.

So if you want to be realistic, if you want to live in reality, then your first thought each morning should be: "thank you for this gift, this new day." And your last thought every evening and in the evening of your life should be: "thank You for this last day, and for all days. I trust You. I believe

16

You are pure love. Your will be done. Love's will be done. My life is Yours; do with it as You will."

One single minute well meant each morning and evening can change your life.

Stay on speaking terms with your Father!

9. What Is "A Good Person"?

We want to be "good" people, and we want those we love to be "good" people. What is a good person? Here is the answer all the great teachers in the world give to that question.

1. A good person is *honest* with himself as well as with others. He refuses the darkness, refuses hiding, and refuses lies. Truth is his absolute.
2. A good person is *unselfish*, self-giving, and generous. There are two kinds of people: givers and grabbers. Be a giver, not a grabber.
3. A good person is *loyal*, trustable, reliable, and responsible. He always keeps his promises.
4. A good person is *moral*. He listens to his conscience. He has an inner life, a character. It's not perfect, but it's there.
5. A good person is *compassionate*. He listens to others' pains, even when they hurt him and upset him. He never turns his back on others.

6. A good person is *humble*, not arrogant. His reaction to bad people is: "There but for the grace of God go I." He never sneers.

7. A good person is *courageous*. He is willing to fight for the good and to suffer for this fight. This virtue is always hard (especially for modern Americans, who have richer and more pain-free lives than anyone in the history of the world) and it takes a long time to cultivate it.

8. A good person is *happy* when he sees others' happiness, happy when he finds beauty, truth, or goodness anywhere. A good person is happy being good.

9. A good person is *obedient*, pious, and reverent and respectful to true and rightful authority, not out of weakness but out of strength.

10. A good person is *grateful*. He knows life is a gift.

10. "Do Your Best"?

An author often gives less than his best to his unknown readers, the anonymous "general public." But no decent parent wants to give anything but his very best to his children.

Yet if we are honest, we must confess that we do not do our best. If you think you do, you are saying that you could not possibly be any better than you are. That sounds impossibly arrogant. In this world none of us do our best, nobody gives all of himself, and nobody never fails. Everybody's glass is partly empty.

But everybody's glass is also partly full. Nobody gives nothing at all. And one of life's happiest lessons is to keep looking for the fullness, not the emptiness, even in people who themselves keep looking at the emptiness, in others or in themselves.

Honest parents know two things: we love our kids like crazy and we don't live out that love as we wish we did. We love and we fail. We love *and* we fail to love.

One way we fail is in courage. We have too many fears. We fear our kids will turn us off, tune us out, or refuse our message because of the flaws in the messenger.

This book is my attempt to remedy that a little. My substitute, my reparation, my penance. Of course a book is no substitute for a person. A book can't be a person. But a book can be personal. It can't be a lover, but it can be a love letter.

11. What I Pray for Every Day

Do you wonder what I pray for you every day? It's the same thing my father prayed for me every day. That you should be happy, really, truly happy.

And therefore good, since there is no other way to be really, truly happy.

And therefore close to God, since He is where all goodness comes from.

12. The Meaning of Life—In One Sentence

Walker Percy said: "Don't get all A's but flunk life."

How do you flunk life?

Leon Bloy said it: "Life offers only one tragedy in the end: not to have been a saint." A saint is one who loves God simply, with whole heart, mind, and soul.

13. What Does "I Love You" Mean?

I know for sure that I love you. But what does that mean?

I don't know that for sure. Love is a great mystery. It's like the ocean: we can only see about ten feet down into it on a clear day.

Love is certainly more than a feeling. I can love you when I have different feelings toward you or have none at all. Feelings are like waves on the sea of love. The sea is still there when there are big waves, little waves, or no waves.

The sea is much heavier than its waves. Love is more than emotion. But not less. It's not cold philanthropy. "I wish you well" is much less than "I love you."

"I love you" means "I tie myself to you." Love is loyal. Love is "no matter what." Love is "never, never, never, never give up."

Because that's what God is like.

14. Time = Life = Family

There are two kinds of time. Abstract time (*kronos* in Greek) is a scientific concept, a way of measuring matter moving through space. Concrete time (*kairos* in Greek) is lived time. We call it our "lifetime." Time is life.

So to give someone your time is to give him your life.

Our families are the ones we give our lives to and the ones who give their lives to us. The family is the "pay-it-forward" institution.

No one was ever heard to say this as he was dying: "I spent too much time with my family and too little time at my work."

Our families always give us more heartbreak than our work because our work isn't big enough to contain our whole heart, as our family is.

What do you do when your family breaks your heart? First, realize this is the way of things, this always happens. Second, mend it. Mend your heart. When you get a broken leg you don't turn away, you mend it. Why? Because you love your leg, because you are your leg. Well, your family is your legs.

15. No Way Out?

Some day you may feel like saying those words to yourself. But they are always false. There is never any problem, misery, or evil in any human relationship that cannot be changed and healed if only two things are present: forgiveness and determination. All the rest is nuts and bolts.

No matter how "incompatible" two people are, they can always "work it out" *if they want to*. The trouble is always *there*: that they don't want to. They'd rather hug their own rightness to their hearts than hug one another.

That's true of our relation to God too. There's only one reason we are not saints: we don't wholly want to be.

You can and will find your way or make your way out of any "impossible" situation if only you begin there: with forgiveness and determination. The only other thing that's always required, after these two, is patience, since all good things take time.

No human relationship is hopeless because no human being is hopeless. Only demons are hopeless.

Amor vincit omnia, "love conquers all." If that's not true, then God's a loser.

16. What Is Honesty?

Honesty is the foundation for all virtues. No virtue can grow in the darkness. Virtues only grow by a kind of spiritual photosynthesis. Light is the universal catalyst for all moral growth, and honesty lets in light.

Honesty with others begins with honesty with yourself. If you play little hide-and-seek games with yourself, you create in yourself the habit of doing that to others. If you don't even respect yourself enough not to lie to yourself, you won't respect others enough not to lie to them.

For honesty, the very first question is always "Is it true?"—even before "Is it good?" For it has to be *truly* good.

And "Is it true?" *certainly* has to be put before "Is it comforting? Is it convenient? Do I like it?" And even more obviously, it has to be put before "Is it popular? Does everybody say so?" Wait! What do *you* say? You're not "everybody." And what does truth say? Truth is not "everybody." *You* should say what *truth* says.

God is truth. Ghandi says: "God is not in strength but in truth."

17. Optimism and Pessimism

Optimism is wrong: evil exists, and life is a war against it.

Pessimism is wrong: good is stronger than evil, and good must win in the end.

So fight, because optimism is wrong. But fight with confidence and even joy, because pessimism is wrong. Fight—don't be a naïve optimist. But fight without fright—don't be a naïve pessimist.

Life is a fight, but the fight is fixed. "His kingdom cannot fail." Life is a play, but there is a script already written. But even though the script is already written, you have to play your part in the play with passion, because life is a passion play.

18. Live in the Present

"Stop and smell the roses." Often. Now. Literally.

Some day it will be too late. Don't wait till it's too late. Read *Our Town* by Thorton Wilder and learn Emily's wisdom after she returns as a ghost. And don't you wait till then!

Living in the present doesn't exclude responsibilities for the future, because those responsibilities are *present*. What it excludes is worry. Worry is living in the future. And that's stupid because the future isn't real.

Here is one of the stupidest philosophies of life I have ever heard, and yet it is the one that drives our whole civilization: it's the idea that the purpose of life is to get good things in the future that you don't yet have, rather than enjoying the good things in the present that you do have. A thousand voices from every corner of our culture whisper that lie. Fight the voices. Command your own thoughts (they're yours to command!) to look at the present and its beauty. If you have to force yourself to stop and smell the roses, well, then, force yourself. Emily's roses are far too beautiful to miss.

Don't listen to advertisements that tell you that you need X or Y or Z. Advertising is the world's oldest profession. The first thing we were sold was a lie and an apple.

What's the one thing people sell all the time but nobody can never buy? God.

19. A Sane Scale of Values

Sanity means living in reality.

Reality isn't just matter. Values are real too, as real as rocks.

Sanity about values means not standing on your head, not living upside down and backwards.

For instance, health is really more valuable than wealth; that's why we pay doctors money. So why do we worry more about money?

And happiness is more valuable than health, as soul is more valuable than body, inner than outer. What we are is more than what we have. So why do we worry more about externals?

And holiness is more valuable than happiness. Being good is more valuable than feeling good. So why do we worry more about our feelings?

⟨∞⟩

20. Self-Esteem

Am I great or what?

Compared with what? With others? Why compare myself with others?

What then is our ground for self-esteem?

That God loved each one of us into existence, by design (He has no unwanted children), and deemed us so important that even when we "no'd" Him, He didn't "no" us but "yes'd" us. In fact, He gave us Himself, His life, and His life's blood; He died so that we could live. He ceased to be so that we could be.

And He didn't do that for "dear occupant," He did it for you. He would have done no less if you had been the only person in the world. In fact, you are the only person in the world, and so am I. That's what love is: when you love someone, that someone is the only person in the world to you. (Remember His parables of God's love: the prodigal son, the lost sheep.) They get 100% of your attention and love, not 10%, or 50%, or 99%. How could God do any less than we do when we love?

He didn't die for humanity. Humanity is an idea, an abstraction, a concept. Fools and politicians talk about dying for concepts; actual soldiers die for their buddies. Humanity doesn't exist. You do. The nail prints in His hands spell out your name.

21. "Mother"

Love your mother. "Mother" means "life-giver." Your mother gave you your live. Literally, physically.

Mother Church gave you spiritual life. God used her as His instrument, as He used your mother. Baptism was your birth canal.

Mother Mary also gave you life by giving you the Life-Giver. The body of Christ is from her body, the blood of Christ is from her blood.

Mother Earth also gave you life, probably by evolution.

You have four mothers. Love them all.

22. What to Do with Time: Some Practical Advice

Amazing how a simple thing like time management can make such a big difference to everything in life.

Amazing how a simple, obvious rule can make such a big difference to time management.

The rule: first work, then play. That way, the work will be done well, unhurried, and without deadlines and time pressures. And the play will be guilt-free and worry-free because your work is done. You know you *deserve* to play now, so you will enjoy it more.

Otherwise, if you play first and then work, the play is full of worry and the work is full of hurry.

23. Sacred Time

Make a sacred, inviolable time each day just to be with the one you love. (I mean both the earthly beloved and the Heavenly Beloved.) Not to *do* anything, just to *be* there.

Nothing should ever be allowed to rob you of your "to-gether-being-time." Better let a thief steal your money than let a thief steal your sacred time, because money isn't life but time is. The thief who steals your money is made of molecules, but the thief who steals your time is made of lies, especially the lie that you have no time to *be*, you always have to *do* something.

Visit a church at least once a week and just spend five minutes in the real presence of Christ in the Blessed Sacrament, just adoring Him. He came a long way for this meeting: all the way from Heaven. And He brought you a long way for this meeting: all the way from nothingness, out of which He created you. He thinks this meeting is that important. And you don't? Which of the two of you do you think has it right?

24. One Minute
To Sanity

One minute isn't enough to get to sanctity, but it is enough to get to sanity. Here's how.

For the sake of your sanity as well as your peace of mind, force yourself to be very quiet and alone with yourself for at least one minute every day. Not one second or one moment but one full minute, sixty seconds. You won't know who's on the inside of your eyeballs if you keep looking away every minute.

When you're feeling the most harried and hassled, deliberately do nothing for one minute. Doing-nothing is very active. It's an act, a doing. It's not doing *nothing*. It's *doing-nothing*. Many people lack the energy it takes to do that.

25. Where the Good Stuff Comes From

"**S**hit happens," says the cynic.

Wrong. It never just happens. Somebody does it. That block of frozen shit that worked its way loose from the rusty airliner toilet, fell 30,000 feet and bashed Grandpa's brains out as he was walking innocently across the Kansas field on that beautiful June day—that didn't just happen.

Good stuff, too, doesn't just happen. Happiness doesn't just happen. Somebody makes it happen.

We say "it rains." What is this "it"? It has to be something. Rain doesn't just happen. *Nothing* "just happens" without a cause, except God. So if you say "shit happens," you're saying that shit is God.

Everything real, good, true, and beautiful and every love, kindness, forgiveness, and self-giving comes from somewhere. And everything unreal, bad, false, ugly, loveless, unkind, unforgiving, and selfish also comes from somewhere. Where?

Look in the mirror.

But there's a difference between the good stuff and the bad stuff: the good stuff comes *through* us. We pass it on, we make it move to others, but where does it come from in the first place? What is the first domino in the chain?

To whatever extent I have passed on goodness to you, you will miss me when I'm gone, because we don't miss badness, only goodness. So if you will miss me when I'm gone, it's important for you to know where the goodness came from, so you can go there and get more of it.

I was a very small, weak, and hesitant domino, a passer-on of the energy of love. But where did it come from? God, of course. And through one single big door: the One who said, "I am the door." All the light in the solar system comes from the sun, and all the light in human life comes from the Son. Many windows, all broken windows, but one light.

Go to the light. That's where I will be, too, being repaired.

26. Laugh!

Contrive somehow to laugh at least once each day. It's medicine. Literally. More important than a vitamin pill. If things are so grim that you can't find anything to laugh at, then laugh at that. A laugh that's half a cry is a good laugh, too.

27. Grudgelessness

"Let not the sun go down upon your wrath." What does that image mean?

Sunset symbolizes death. Life is too short for grudges. We can die any day. And we can never repair the break if we die at war instead of at peace.

Don't go to sleep when you're still at war.

28. What's the Big Deal about Church?

Why is she so important?

Because she is how we know Jesus. She tells us (by her teaching), shows us (by her saints), and feeds us (by her sacraments).

Why is Jesus so important?

Because He is how we know God. He told us, showed us, and fed us.

Why is God so important?

Because He is how we know love. He IS love.

Why is love so important?

Because it's how we know happiness.

Without love, our happiness is not true happiness.

Without God, our love is not true love.

Without Jesus, our God is not the true God.

Without the Church, our Jesus is not the true Jesus.

29. Something about Sex

First, let's start with something you know already. Sex is good, sex is great. God made it such a joy because He's just brimming over with joy. And He glued this most ecstatic joy to the most godlike power we have, the power to (pro-)create new people, new immortals.

Second, this God of ecstasies is behind all the right rules about it. There's really only one: no adultery. Don't adulterate this, don't water down this drink. The most basic rule is embarrassingly easy to understand: it's for marriage. In marriage, yes, in fact, sex to the max; outside marriage, no.

Jews and Muslims have the same rule. It came from the Designer. If it didn't, if the commandments aren't from God Himself, then the whole Bible is a fraud, and so is the whole Christian religion, including our hope of Heaven. If it isn't God speaking there but only ourselves, what hope do we have? Can we pull ourselves up to Heaven by our own bootstraps?

Third, the sexual revolution has already destroyed more families and more human happiness than any political revolution in history (with the possible exception of the one in 1917). Listen to Dr. Laura's talk show: every single distraught caller bleeds from the same wound, inflicted by the same Clintonesque prick. Don't be one. Not just because it's forbidden but because it's fake.

Remove sex from the place it's designed to live in; remove it from total love, commitment, self-giving, and fidelity; remove it from marriage, family, children, and society; turn it into a private, "consensual," "libertarian," "recreational" thing; and what do you have? Something like the consecrated Eucharist used for a fluffernutter sandwich. Mutual masturbation. Loving fantasy pictures instead of real persons.

Fake sex doesn't make for true happiness. Deep down everybody knows that. But we don't want to know it. We want to make ourselves stupid. We haven't been thinking too much about sex, we've been thinking too little. Fantasizing isn't thinking.

We need truth about everything, therefore we need truth about sex. We need light about the fire. Light comes from the head, not the heart or the hormones.

Once we think honestly, everything else follows. All morality is based on thinking honestly.

30. Modern Times

These are hard times for children because they are hard times for childhood. Our civilization is killing childhood. One way it's doing that is by killing the thing that was enjoyed by most kids in America, especially in summer: leisure. Even that is now programmed.

It's also destroying families. The womb kids grow in is not just inside the mother but outside, too: it's called the family. These two wombs are supposed to be the safest, happiest, and most nurturing places on earth. But in our civilization, they are the two most dangerous, deadly, and traumatic places on earth.

One out of every three or four children conceived in America is murdered in the womb of the mother by abortion. That is as shocking as one out of every three or four born people are being murdered, because "a person's a person no matter how small."

The basis of the family is marriage. One out of every two marriages commits suicide by divorce. That is as shocking as half of all individuals committing suicide, because the basic units of a society are not individuals but families.

And most violence happens in families. Most murders of born people are by family members or boyfriends. Both wombs, both places of security, have become dangerous and deadly.

Even financially, children in our society are felt as a burden rather than the asset they were in all previous societies. How unnatural that young married couples typically have to choose between a house *or* children—or moving to Iowa. Mothers have to work and rent a mother-substitute for day care. This is progress?

But even when our bad economic system makes kids financial "burdens," they are still personal pleasures. For while money diminishes when shared, love multiples. Spirit and matter follow opposite laws. Altruism divides your income but multiplies your outgo; it divides your money but multiplies your love and your happiness if you're sane enough to pin that happiness to your love rather than to your money.

31. What Is a Family?

Our "experts" don't even know any more what everybody else knows: what a family is. They demand not just toleration for nonfamilies—that's good—but redefinition of the family so that nonfamilies can be families—and that's bad, because it's not true.

If two gays or lesbians can be a family, why not three? Why not four spouse swappers? Why not polygamy? Why don't I have the right to redefine the family so that I can marry my sheep? The question is a serious, logical question and demands a serious, logical answer. Why not? We already have cloning, surrogate mothers, test-tube babies, and more. We can have *Brave New World* tomorrow. Read the book; it's prophetic.

Without stable familes, where do we learn what love is? Where else are you loved not because you give amusement or sexual pleasure or economic benefit, but just for who you are, not for what you do?

I remember once when you were small, one of you asked me, after you had failed at something or other, "Daddy, do you love me?" "I sure do," I said. But you asked, "Why do you love me?" My answer was: "Because I'm your Daddy. Because you're mine." It's so simple and so obvious why we need families.

Nothing hurts kids more than broken families. And nothing is more selfish and irresponsible and inexcusable than hurting kids. Especially *your* kids.

The most horrible way our society hurts kids is by literally tearing them limb from limb, sucking their brains out, burning their skin off, crushing their skulls, and breaking their bones.

That's what the "procedure" of abortion does. We do that to a quarter of all the children we conceive. I cannot understand how "civilized" human beings can tolerate that. Almost no one who *sees* it, who faces its sheer physical reality, can tolerate it. Babies in a dumpster, nine-month-old, perfectly-formed babies, our babies—the photos bear an eerie resemblance to the emaciated, naked bodies of the Jews whom the Nazis redefined as "nonpersons" and bulldozed into mass graves.

What can conquer this evil? Only strong, sacrificial love. Arguments alone can't change hearts. Love can.

We have been given a love that lasts forever, from the only One who lasts forever: a love that is not an affair of the moment or the month but of eternity. The world does not believe in this love any more. You have to show it to them. You have to help Him save the world.

Strange indeed that He would use such imperfect instruments as us to help Him save the world. Strange indeed that He would use such an imperfect instrument as me to love you.

32. Only One Thing Necessary

I don't care whether you're rich or poor, only that you're good.

You don't even have to be smart (though you are), you just have to be good.

You don't even have to be beautiful (though you are), just good.

You don't even have to be successful. If you were poor and stupid and ugly but good, you'd be successful. If you were rich and smart and beautiful but evil, you'd be a failure. Why? Because good is what real is, good is what God is.

It doesn't even matter much (not as much as we usually think) whether others are good to you. What matters most is whether you are good to them. For you aren't responsible for others' free choice to be good to you; they are. And they aren't responsible for your free choice to be good to them; you are.

33. How to Be a Good Person: Step One

Step one is to stop pretending that you are one.

There are only two kinds of people: sinners, who think they're saints, and saints, who know they're sinners. There are only fools, who think they are wise, and the wise, who know they are fools.

Step one for many people in our society is to stop being so insufferably "self-affirming," to stop listening to the self-righteous prigs who give us advice on how to be self-righteous prigs, and to stop "accepting yourself as you are." That's what toddlers do.

34. Step Two: Ten Ways to Be a Good Person

There are ten commandments that define what it is to be a good person. They're God's ideas about us, not our ideas about God.

1. "You shall have no other gods before me." Being good means being loyal to persons and first of all to God, the Original Person and the Inventor and Creator of all persons.

   Muslims wisely repeat five times a day, "there is no God but God." (*La illa'ha 'illa Allah!*") Worship God or nothing, because nothing else is God.

2. "You shall not take the name of the Lord your God in vain." Words are sacred. By His word, God created the universe. "In the beginning was the word."

   As we speak, so we think; and as we think, so we live; and as we live, so we are. If you care about who you are, care about how you speak.

Be honest with words. Speak truly. And be good to words, *love* true words. Sing beautiful music when you speak.

Three names of God that we must not take in vain are truth, goodness, and beauty.

3. "Remember the Sabbath day, to keep it holy." Take sabbaticals. Learn the art of leisure. Learn to relax and enjoy God's gifts. And learn to enjoy God: "be still and know that I am God."

   If you do this, you will learn that God is not a boss but a Father, and that we are not His worker bees but His kids.

   This will make everything different. For instance, we will see that the universe is His toy box for us, and that the ocean is a perfect toy: always there, always willing to play with you, just dangerous enough to be exciting, never needing replacement, unbreakable, never boring, and you don't even have to put it away when you're finished playing with it. Watch how little kids treat it; they know what it's for. They also know what snow and rain are for.

   Be an adult only six days out of seven. "All work and no play makes Jack a dull boy." We know we have to work, but we forget we have to play. Poor God: He doesn't have to command us to work, but He has to command us to play!

4. "Honor your father and your mother." The family is God's invention and God's image: the Trinity is a family. It's sacred.

Tradition is humanity's extended family. Like your nuclear family, it's far from perfect, but even its mistakes are precious because they're yours. We can learn from them. Learn from all your parents, back to Adam.

5. "You shall not murder." "Choose life" because human life isn't just *good*, it's *sacred*.

Don't fall for the con job of calculating the value of life. Deep down, everyone knows life is sacred, even when defaced by pain or death or even sin. Don't fall for propaganda like "quality time" or "quality of life." "Quality time" is used as an excuse for not giving your kids as much of your time (= your life) as you know you ought to give them. And "quality of life" is used as an excuse for killing people who aren't as healthy as their killers.

6. "You shall not steal." Since people are sacred, their bodies are too. And since their bodies are sacred, so are their extended bodies, their "stuff," their possessions. Others' possessions are to be respected. People are to be loved. God is to be worshipped.

Worship God, love people, and respect stuff.

Respect all three, love people and God but not stuff, and worship God alone.

Don't worship people or stuff, and don't love stuff.

Things are means, not ends. Things are to be used, people are ends to be loved. We are really stupid, because unless we remember to correct ourselves, we naturally slide into using people and loving things. We continually have to remind ourselves to be sane, to live in reality, to treat everything as what it really is. If we don't do this, we will always bump up against the wall of reality, and no paint will come off that wall but some flesh will come off our face.

The point of the sixth commandment is that although things are not to be worshipped or loved, they are to be respected. When a person makes a thing *his* thing, that thing acquires a claim on us to respect because it is now his. We are commanded to respect others' stuff and space.

7. "You shall not commit adultery." Marriage is God's self-portrait. The holy family on earth (Jesus, Mary, and Joseph) is an image of the holy family in Heaven, the Trinity. The Trinity is a perfect marriage, totally unadulterated. Marriage is the most godlike human relation possible in this world. It can't be perfect, but it can be unadulterated.

Nothing is more sacred than marriages, not even churches. If all churches went very bad but all marriages became very good, that would be a better world than one in which all marriages went bad but churches remained good.

Never, never betray your spouse, because that is betraying yourself, your honor, and your honesty.

What you do with your body, you do with God's body if you are a baptized Christian, baptized into "the body of Christ."

Marriage is as sacred as the Eucharist, because it's a different form of the same thing: the body of Christ. Adulterating it is like using the sacred Host as a Frisbee. Killing it by divorce is killing Christ.

See, this is Big Stuff, Serious Stuff, capital-letter stuff. We're in way over our heads, swimming in giant waves, and if we don't use God's flotation devices, we will wipe out and drown.

8. "You shall not bear false witness against your neighbor." Lying is the clearest violation of the golden rule: "do unto others what you want others to do unto you." You don't want to be lied to. Nobody does. Therefore, don't lie.

   This is an extremely practical, efficient commandment: if you live in the light, a million messes will be cleaned up. If you live in the dark, you'll keep stumbling over the hidden garbage.

   Like all sins, lies put on disguises. (The devil has to put bait on his hooks.) They *look* like safety, or profit, or fun, or escapes. But lies are *lies*. See through their disguises. God made you Superman-like, gave you x-ray vision with the Ten Commandments.

   Obeying this commandment completely will lead to obeying all the other ones. For all sin is a lack of honesty. All sin covers-up. Stop covering-up. Love the light. Live in the light, and you'll stop sinning.

   The clearest light comes when you die. There aren't many sins a person will commit on his deathbed.

   How do you get that clarity? Practice.

   Speak only truth. But gently. Don't bear false witness *or* true witness *against* your neighbor.

9. "You shall not covet your neighbor's wife." Lust is a drug. Be clean of drugs. Be free. Addicts aren't free.

After each relapse, go cold turkey. No compromises. "Just say no," first of all to the thought. "But thoughts aren't as bad as deeds." Wrong; deliberate thoughts *are* deeds: deeds of thought, choices.

Thoughts aren't so bad? "Sow a thought, reap and act; sow an act, reap a habit; sow a habit, reap a character, sow a character, reap a destiny."

Buddha knew that. "All that we are is shaped by our thoughts. It begins where our thoughts begin, it moves where our thoughts move, it ends where our thoughts end."

Saying no to the thought, earlier, is a lot easier than saying no to the act, later, after you've already welcomed the thought into your mind's house. It's harder to evict a resident tenant than to turn aside an applicant at the door.

Of course we're all weak. But God provides constant rehab. But He doesn't force it on you.

10. "You shall not covet your neighbor's goods." How stupid to covet others' stuff. God made plenty of stuff to go around.

Envy is the stupidest sin of all. It never gave anyone a minute of even false happiness.

Envy of others' riches (coveting money) is even stupider, because it confuses the *end* we all seek with a *means* of exchange.

35. Step Three: The Payoff

All virtue makes you happy. All sin makes you miserable.

The only obstacle to virtue and, therefore, happiness is sin.

The only thing that can conquer sin is God's grace—twice: before you sin, to prevent it, and after you sin, to forgive it. Both are grace, but the second is much more costly to God. See the movie.

Gifts are freely given and freely received. God's gift of forgiveness is received only by our own free choice to repent. Repentance includes two free choices: a no and a yes: No to sin and yes to God. It is the free choice to "convert," to "turn"—away from sin and to God.

God gives grace, the grace to conquer sin. But He gives that gift gradually, not instantly. (But you should see some progress.) He does it from within: He actually lives in our souls personally in the person of the Holy Spirit. He is called "the Sanctifier," which means "the saint-maker."

We can't do it without Him and He won't do it without us. He gives us the power but He doesn't do it for us. Grace doesn't replace nature, human nature, or human choice, but perfects it and energizes it.

God is not like us. God is not a lawyer or a legalist. He's not hung up on our past sins, any more than a good doctor is hung up on past diseases. Like a good doctor, He tells us preventative measures so we can worry less. But medicine isn't the end, only the means. (This is true of spiritual medicine as well as physical medicine.) The end is health. That means that avoiding sin and obeying the commandments, tremendously important as it is, is not the final end of life but only a necessary means. The end is love and joy. That's the end because that's what God is.

⚜

36. Life Is Art

Each human life is a statue, or a picture, or a poem, or a song. Your life is one, too.

Every work of art has two parts: the matter and the form. The matter is what comes to you, the form is what comes from you. The matter of your life is the raw material you inherit through heredity and environment. The form is how you shape that matter by your choices to make the unique story that is your life.

What you inherit is like a fence around a playground: it limits your choices. You can't change your century, your gender, or your parents. But it also makes your choices possible. Without a fence, no playground: you'd be out in the street.

Life gives everybody some lemons, but only some people make good lemonade. One person is served fine wine and spills it; another is served old grapes and makes his own wine with a lot of stomping and testing. The part we contribute (the form) is more important than the part nature contributes (the matter, the raw material, the opportunities).

⚜

37. The Four Most Important Choices of Your Life

The four most important choices you make are the ones that make the biggest difference to your life: a God to believe in, a mate to marry, friends to be with, and a career to work at. You give your life to each of them in different ways.

Make these choices wisely. For they are not only the tools by which you shape your life, they are also the tools by which your life shapes you.

These four choices aren't equal. They are in a hierarchy. No matter how important your job is, it's not a person. No matter how important friends are, they don't give you your kids. No matter how great your mate is, he or she can't save your soul.

So don't worship your job, or your friends, or your spouse. And don't marry your friends or your job. And don't feel betrayed by your job.

38. Three Idols

It sounds strange to speak (as I did above) of "choosing" a God to worship, as if you were in a Chinese restaurant ordering gods, "one from column A and two from column B." But I don't mean just choosing a church or even a religion but choosing an absolute. God's very first commandment is "Have no other gods before me." And the very last command of the very last apostle (John) was: "Little children, keep yourselves from idols." (John 5:11) Anything can become an idol, a false god, even a paper clip collection if you're Bert on Sesame Street.

The three most popular idols are money, sex, and power. The three deadliest of the seven deadly sins are greed, lust, and pride. These are the three main sources of evil, "the world, the flesh, and the devil." That's why monks take three vows: poverty, chastity, and obedience.

We need money, sex, and power. They are good, not evil. But they are good because God invented them. Putting them first and God second is putting the invention above the Inventor.

We all do that. We're all very, very stupid. So God has to remind us, over and over (He never gives up!), sometimes painfully. He has to slap our hands free from them when we grasp them so tightly that we hurt our own hands and hearts. When we become addicts, God has to become our drug rehab therapist.

39. One Gift for You

Suppose God came down the chimney this Christmas instead of Santa Claus and said to me, "I'll give you any one gift. Anything you ask. Guaranteed. What do you want?" What would I ask for?

First of all, I'd ask it for *you*.

Then, I'd ask for Heaven.

My worst hell would be to go to Heaven and not find you there. To wander across Heaven forever searching for you and not finding you would turn my Heaven into Hell.

Woody Allen says that the most important thing in life is showing up. That's the most important thing in the afterlife, too.

I hope you know how to get to Heaven, how to have a happy eternity. There is a way, and the way is a person, the one who said "I AM the way." (John 14:6) God gave us a well-marked road map, the Bible. Both this person and this book are called "the word of God."

I hope you are very, very clear about this. Your catechism teachers, your theology courses, and your parents should have been very, very clear about that but probably weren't. We get too hung up on big second things and forget the biggest thing of all, the first thing.

Please don't be insulted by this very elementary reminder: it's not you but your teachers that I'm insulting, first of all myself.

40. How Do You Get to Heaven from Here?

The answer is *not* the punch line of the classic Vermont farmer joke: "Ya can't get there from here."

According to the Ticket Master, it's a two-part ticket. We need to do two things to get there from here: "repent and believe." "Repenting" means detaching ourselves from the train that's going in the opposite direction and "believing" means attaching ourselves to the train that's going to Heaven.

"Repent" is the one-word summary of all the prophets in the Bible. Repent of what? Of sin, of "no's" to God. Everyone needs to repent because everyone is a sinner. There are only two kinds of people: unrepentant sinners and repentant sinners.

"Believe" means "trust." Its object is not merely an idea but a person. All ideas come from persons (they certainly don't come from the sky or from the ground), and we believe some people's ideas only because we trust *them*. (And God is a person. "I AM" is His name.)

The scientific method rightly tells us to treat all ideas as guilty until proven innocent, false until proven true. That's a good method for science but a bad method for life, a good method for ideas but a bad method for persons. (And God is a Person.)

The world says: "Don't trust anybody. Play it safe. If you give your heart away, it will be broken. If you give your mind away, it will be deceived. Trust only yourself. Look out for number one."

God says: "I'm your Father. I love you, I want to bless you. Trust me. Hope in me. I fulfill all my promises, in my time, which is the best time, and in my way, which is the best way. I promise you Heaven: all that you desire, all that you *can* desire, more than you desire, more than you can desire, more than you can imagine. Hitch your wagon to my star."

He also tells us that the secret of our happiness (as of His) is to give your heart away, to give your life away, to give your self away, in love. Because that's what He did for us. Sure, your heart will be broken, but it will beat, it will be alive, it will grow. The only whole heart is the broken heart.

Even Rodney Dangerfield warns you: "While you're looking out for number one, you're going to step on a lot of number two." Remember what "number two" meant when you were two.

41. Honor

The word used to make us look up. Now it makes us look down, because we either understand it and are ashamed of ourselves for not living up to it, or else we misunderstand it and confuse it with snobbery, and look down on it. And that looking-down on honor is itself snobbery, because honor is a looking-up.

Honor means having excellence in yourself (being honorable) or admiring excellence in another (honoring another). Excellence is not snobbery. Only people who are dishonorable, resentful, and envious see excellence as snobbery. Only snakes sneer at eagles.

Today we're honored and admired not for being different, better, excellent, but for *not* being different.

Honor is not necessarily competitive. We often think it is because one of the few parts of life today that still understands the striving for excellence is competitive sports.

We honor heroes. We used to have heroes, now we have only sports heroes. They don't even teach the lives of the saints in religion classes any more.

Maybe that's why we're so fascinated with the Nazis. Why are they so much more interesting than the communists, whose leaders and whose deeds were just as wicked, and who murdered ten times more innocent people? Maybe it's because the communists told the world they were all equal and machines, while the Nazis told the Germans they were a super-race of gods. Insane and wicked but interesting.

Honor honor.

42. Life as Fetal Rehearsals

Socrates thought of philosophy as something that came from life and was meant for life, not something that came from books and was meant for books. And this thing (philosophy) that meant "the love of wisdom" he called "a rehearsal (*melete*) for dying."

He was righter than he realized. For love is a kind of dying—to self, to egotism. And the life we are destined for forever in Heaven is a life of eternal, blissful, self-giving, dying-to-self love. The reason that's so is because "that's *so*," that's the way it is, that's the nature of ultimate reality (God): a Trinity of eternal, blissful, dying-to-self, self-giving love. And in Heaven, we will be utterly real, utterly in tune with ultimate reality.

The meaning of life on earth is rehearsal for *that*. All the stuff about morality is so much more than propriety and safety; it's learning to surf on that divine sea without wiping out.

A fetus doesn't understand why it has eyes and feet. Why is it kicking? There's nothing hard in the womb to kick against. It's rehearsing for the great day of birth. And so are we.

43. Mornings

Heraclitus said "the sun is new every day." He was astronomically wrong but spiritually right. Each day is a new gift from God. It doesn't come from yesterday. It comes from God. Time can't make more time. Only God can make more time. Thank Him for it every morning.

We think mornings happen automatically only because of habit, like children getting allowances.

One morning, there *won't* be another morning.

44. Some Maxims

1. Thank God for everything. *Everything.*
2. Forgive everything. *Everything.*
3. Be ready and willing at every moment to die, to lose everything. *Everything.*
4. Be a realist. Live in reality. Therefore, love God as He really is: *Everything.*
5. Hold back nothing from Him. *Nothing.*
6. Fear nothing but the loss of Him. *Nothing.*
7. When you have nothing left for yourself, you will have nothing to fear. *Nothing.*
8. Having God, you have everything. *Everything.*
9. Don't even *contemplate* compromises. Adulterate nothing. *Nothing.*
10. How much time each day should we spend praying? 24 hours. *Everything.*

45. Divine Grace and Human Freedom

When things go wrong, especially when we know it was our own fault, we naturally ask whether this was because God didn't give us the grace or because He did, but we didn't use it aright. And this brings up the great mystery of the interplay between our activity and God's, between free will and God's grace.

For thousands of years, the greatest philosophers and theologians have only given us partial solutions, helpful hints. No one has removed the mysteriousness of the mystery, and probably no one ever will. We just don't know how grace "works" any more than a baby knows how electricity works.

Why hasn't God solved this puzzle for us? Because God is not in the puzzle-solving business. Instead of explaining to us how the "electricity" of His grace works, He gave us the "off" and "on" buttons and told us to push the "on" buttons of faith, hope, love, and prayer. Instead of explaining it, He provided it. He gave us food, not a gastrointestinal physiology textbook.

Why haven't we solved the puzzle? Because it's not a puzzle to be solved but a mystery to be lived.

And because if He did show up (as He did to Job) and gave us the very best answer we could possibly understand (as He did to Job), it would probably sound something like this (as it did to Job): "Hush, my little one. You couldn't possibly understand. Just trust me."

When we philosophize about grace and freedom we usually forget the lived *context* of the problem: it's "all in the family." Daddy tells Baby all Baby needs to know about electricity: turn the lights off and on by these switches and don't stick metal in plugs.

He has told us the two things we most need to know about grace. He hasn't told us much about philosophy—about impersonal, theoretical truth—but He has told us whom to praise and whom to blame, because those are personal and practical things.

First, whom to praise: all good is grace, all good comes from God, no matter how long and hidden the chain of instruments He uses to get it to us. Ultimately, everything is grace. Nature itself is grace; it's the nature of grace. So we should give God all the credit for all the good that exists, because He's where it all comes from. He's not just all-good, He's the Creator of all good, including your very existence. Being created is sheer grace because no one can ever deserve to be created; how could you deserve anything when you don't even exist?

Second, whom to blame: no evil comes from God. If it did, He'd be part-God and part-devil. Evil comes from us. We can't create, but we can destroy. Much good comes from us, too, but only because it comes from Him first, and because "grace perfects nature" and, therefore, also human nature.

If any grace is good for us, God does not withhold that grace from us. Either He offers it and we refuse it (out of fear, ignorance, pride, or whatever), or He withholds it because He sees that it wouldn't really be best for us. St. Thomas says that God is like a doctor who deliberately refuses to cure a lesser ailment because of the danger of contracting a greater one. So He doesn't give us the grace to conquer some lesser but obvious sin to prevent us from the greater sin of hidden pride, which would harm us even more.

46. Money

Money is not bad. Greed is. It's not true that "money is the root of all evil." That's not what the Bible says; it says that "the love of money is the root of all kinds of evils."

Only persons are to be loved. Loving only people wonderfully simplifies our life, frees us up, and liberates us from the billions of little things we worry about, like pennies. (Ten million dollars is only a billion pennies.)

When someone we love is dying, we know that money is nothing. We'd all rather be alive and poor than rich and dead. And we'd rather be in love in the South Bronx than fighting in Hawaii and rather be married in a tent than divorced in a mansion.

47. Style

If the style of a book turns me off, I don't read it, no matter what it's about. And if an author has a totally trustable style, like C. S. Lewis, I'll read his book no matter what it's about.

I think this applies to people as well as books and to style of speaking and living as well as writing. I think "body language" is like writing style: it reveals more than it says.

I've found that of all the books I've written the most appreciated are the ones with the simplest, most user-friendly style, reader-oriented rather than author-oriented. I can write more cleverly, even more "brilliantly," but that's a performance, not an operation. A book should be an operation; it should be heart surgery. Stylistic cleverness is for the author. It says: "Look at me, look at my work." Stylistic transparency and simplicity and economy is for the reader. It says: "Look at this, look *through* what I say, at the truth and at yourself." That's true of writing style and of living style, too.

48. The Oprah Piss Test

I read *Tuesdays with Morrie*, a book many of my friends loved, but it left me cold. The author is a nice man, but he's too nice. He didn't honestly confront the big, tough questions. When a man is dying, you want to know how he faces his God and his eternity and his future. But the only books about dying that get our media's approvals are the ones written by agnostics.

No, that's not right. What bothered me about the book was not its agnosticism but its self-satisfaction. Camus was an agnostic, but far from self-satisfied. Scott Peck's *The Road Less Travelled* was (or seemed) agnostic, but it was powerful because it was honest and tough-minded instead of tender-minded. (The two very useful categories come from William James, another tough-minded agnostic.) *Tuesdays with Morrie* would never piss off Oprah. That's my test for a Great Book: The Oprah Piss Test.

Honest agnostics are always in danger of making a leap of faith. Some make it before they die. Camus didn't, but he was moving up that road. The "religiously correct" media establishment is uncomfortable with honest agnostics because it sees where that road leads. That's why it prefers less honest agnostics who aren't moving anywhere (and who therefore praise "change" and "openness" without specifying where the change is going or what the openness is open to). What they mean is change in any direction except truth and openness to openness but not to truth. C. S. Lewis had them pegged. It's all in chapter 5 of *The Great Divorce*.

49. Simplicity

Everyone today complains that life is too complex. Everyone yearns for simplicity. There are ways to simplify your life. I suggested a few external ways in the chapter on simplicity in *Making Choices*. But it has to start with internal simplification.

On the intellectual level, that can be done by looking at a wonderfully simple piece of advice from St. Thomas Aquinas. He says there are only three kinds of goods: the morally good, the practically good, and the delightful good (*bonum honestum, bonum necessacium, bonum delicabile*). So there are only three good reasons to do anything: because it's morally good (an act of justice, virtue, charity, or heroism), because it's a practical necessity (like eating or making enough money to eat), or because it makes you happy. That's it. Period. How many things do we do that are none of those three? Stop doing them. Throw the excess cargo overboard. Lighten the ship. It's sinking with all that extra weight.

On the level of the will, love, and the desires, the most important simplifying principle of all is that life has only one good, one end, point, purpose, goal, meaning, and perfection, like the point of an arrow, and only if we come to the point of knowing and seeking that end, can we be like an arrow and come to a point. Only if we have one great love, can we be one great person. If our loves are dissipated, so are we. If they are one, so are we.

In the Bible, poor Martha was "anxious and worried about many things." She sounds familiar. Jesus told her that "only one thing is necessary." What a radical liberation! Only one thing! If you don't know what that one thing is, read John's Gospel again.

I just read a newspaper account of a Danish prince who came back from an expedition by dogsled across the Greenland icecap. Asked what he found most exhilarating about the trip, he replied, "The freedom."

The sharpest arrow of all was Mary, who boiled down all of life into one word: *"fiat,"* "yes." You can be the greatest success in the world just by knowing and doing this Mary thing. That's the total opposite of vague, sweetly pious idealism. It's the most hard-headed, practical calculation you can make. For "what does it profit a man to gain the whole world and lose his own self?" Could anyone ever say a more practical sentence than that?

Our culture makes this practicality impractical, makes this simplicity anything but simple, by throwing itself around us like an enormous spiderweb. And then, if a fly does escape its meshes, it throws nasty names at it like "simplistic" and "narrow-minded" and "fanatical" (the culture's F-word). Of course, it's none of those things. It's simply happiness. But the culture is jealous of a happiness it can't understand or produce. So it resorts to sneer words.

50. Emptiness

I want to leave most of this page empty to remind you that your spirit needs emptiness and silence. If there's no emptiness in you, there's no room in you for anything—like a certain inn in Bethlehem. He often knocks at the door of our inns, wearing many disguises. Save a room for Him.

51. Lesson
from a Great Poet

Thomas Carlyle (died 1881) was a great English poet. He loved his wife, she loved him, and helped him in his career. But she fell ill with cancer and was bedridden, and Thomas was so busy writing that he rarely made time to stay at her bedside. But she did not complain.

After she died, it rained heavily on the day of her burial. After the ceremony at the graveside, Thomas went home, went up into his wife's bedroom, and sat beside her bed. He found her diary, and read this entry: "Yesterday Thomas spent an hour with me and it was like being in Heaven. I love him so." His heart quaked. On the next page he read: "I have listened all day to hear his steps in the hall, but now it is late and I guess he won't come today."

Thomas threw the diary to the floor and ran back to the cemetery through pouring rain. Friends found him face down in the mud on the new grave, weeping, saying over and over again, "If only I had known!"

Woody Allen is right: "Ninety percent of life is just showing up."

52. Stop and Smell the Roses

L iterally.

Smelling roses is more beautiful, more happifying, and more heavenly than half the things we do instead, the things we pass the roses by for. Most of the time we choose mechanical roses instead of real ones.

We strut and fret and preen and pose, but only God can make a rose.

53. Love's Logic

Love has eyes. Perfect love has perfect eyes, perfect wisdom. God is perfect wisdom *because* He is perfect love.

Love also has power, and God also is perfect power *because* He is perfect love.

God gives us everything we need because that's what love does. He's able to do it because He has perfect power, and He knows what to do because He has perfect wisdom.

But it doesn't look like we're getting all we need. So we have to take our choice: to believe our wisdom or His.

Appearances deceive. Diseases, divorces, depressions, deceptions, deaths—a formidable array of appearances. Where is God?

Not in the appearances. Deeper.

Realer.

Closer.

54. How to Make It Easy to Be Good

It's very simple: make people happy, really happy, because that makes *you* happy, and when you're happy, it's easier to be good.

55. Temptations of Old Age

When you're young, you're tempted to be selfish and irresponsible and forget others' misery in the demand to enjoy yourelf. When you're old, you're tempted to be unselfish and responsible and to make others miserable by never enjoying yourself.

Epitaph by C. S. Lewis: "Erected by her sorrowing brothers/In memory of Martha Clay/Here lies one who lived for others/Now she has peace. And so have they."

56. The Highest Wisdom

The highest wisdom is also the lowest, the simplest, the most obvious, and the most well-known. It is the knowledge that the meaning of life is love.

Honest love, true love, unconditional love, simple love. Love of the other for the other's sake, not yours; love as an end in itself, not a means to the end of return-love; not a bargain, not a performance for rewards. Love that's self-forgetful and thus, paradoxically, self-fulfilling.

Sometimes we understand this but don't do it. But sometimes we do it even when we don't understand it. Wisdom consists not in knowing it but in doing it.

All the religions of the world know some form of the great secret, "lose yourself to find it." Christianity knows its ultimate source: that God is love, that God is a Trinity of persons in which each person gives Himself to the others. The more we do that, the more real we become.

57. Forgiving

Why must we forgive all offenses? Because we have been forgiven all offenses by the One whom we offend in all offenses. ("Whatever you do to one of the least of these, my family, you do to me.")

And because that One tells us that we cannot be forgiven unless we forgive.

Why? Not because God withholds it. He doesn't. But we cannot receive it, even though He gives it, when the hands of our souls are closed.

When we don't forgive others, we make them our masters. When we chew on others' faults, we make them the masters of our misery.

If we forgive only the forgivable and not the unforgivable, if we proportion our love to dessert, then we subject love to justice. And that is idolatry, for God is love. Justice is only love's backup. When love is gone, justice is needed to protect us from each other.

Forgive everyone.
Forgive everything.
Forgive always.
Forgive everywhere.
Why? Because God does. You can't enjoy God's Heaven until you're like God. That's what purgatory is for: enjoyment.

58. One Word

One single word is more than all the other words in this book and in all other books ever written. That one word is the meaning of life and all our hope and joy. The word is Jesus. Other words are our words; He is "God's word," God's single word to us. Instead of speaking speeches, God speaks Jesus.

Jesus is not an *example* of truth or goodness or beauty or anything else. He is not a *teacher* of truth or goodness or beauty. He IS truth and goodness and beauty, "the way, and the truth, and the life." He is universal truth, goodness, and beauty incarnated in the particular.

59. Jesus the Comedian

Jesus had a fantastic sense of humor. Even if you don't detect it in the Gospels (but how can you miss it?), you can detect it in nature. He's the mind ("logos") of God who designed nature, after all. How can you look at a basset hound and not know Jesus is a comedian? And some of those deep-sea fish—absolutely over the top and off the wall.

The two greatest jokes of all time were the incarnation and the crucifixion. They were the two great jokes God played on the devil. The incarnation was the great disappearing act and the crucifixion was the great judo act.

Even if you don't get it now, you will in Heaven, where you will have the last laugh forever.

60. Lord Truth

Lord Truth is "the one thing necessary." If you stand in His presence, if you turn the face of your mind to Him, then nothing evil can come between you and Him because between your face and His there is then only light, and nothing evil can survive light.

Never run from truth. Never turn away. Always face truth, face the light. Love it, even when it seems painful.

Honesty is the very first virtue because on it all others depend. Compromise this, and all the others are compromised. Ugly worms begin to creep out of holes in your soul. Only the light drives them back.

God is light. We must learn to become totally light-friendly because He is inescapable, and we have to either endure or enjoy that "being of light" forever. After death there will be no more darkness and no more hiding.

So be prepared to pay any price to kill those little worms. There are many of them.

Lord Truth has many servants acting like knights who will ride out to kill the little worms and even the big dragons if we only ask them to come. Some of the names of these knights are Honor, Justice, Listening, Openness, Courage, Self-control, and Wisdom.

Honesty with others begins with honesty with yourself. Lie to yourself, and you will necessarily lie to others. One lie covers up another.

And honesty with yourself begins with honesty with God. You are never all alone; when you are alone with yourself, you are in the presence of God. For God is truth.

Truth is not a cold lord. He is a volcano of love. Truth is not correctness; truth is God.

Lord Truth will bring you to Lord Goodness, and Lord Goodness will bring you to Lord Beauty, who is also Lord Joy.

The order is not reversible. We cannot get joy and beauty at the expense of goodness, though we often seem to. (That's the devil's most successful lie—that sin is fun.) And we cannot get goodness at the expense of truth, though we often seem to. (That's the devil's second most successful lie—that goodness doesn't have to be true goodness, just felt goodness.)

Serving Lord Truth is serving Jesus, whether you know it or not. For Jesus said, "I AM the truth." Socrates, Ghandi, Moses, and Mohammed did not know that; Christians do. Because Lord Truth is a person, you have to ask Lord Truth to rule you. For He is a He, not an "it." He will not come if you do not want Him, and He will come if you do.

Please do.

61. The Four Dimensions

Everything we do has four dimensions.

The one we see is the length: how long it takes to do a job, how big a material object is. This is the material, visible, external, outer, this-worldly, natural dimension. We are created to work with and in this dimension, to shape wood and space into statues, and sound and time into song.

This dimension is quite real, but as an adjective, not a noun: it is not reality as such but a dimension of reality. It is not another, lower, lesser *world*, like a cellar or a cave. Though it is material, it shares in the honor of the three other dimensions, which are spiritual, as the body shares in the honor of the soul and as the molecules of a painting share in its meaning and beauty.

The second dimension is the *height*: the relationship to the "higher power," to God, however inadequately He is known. (And we must admit that He is always inadequately known, once we stop fooling ourselves.)

The whole universe is a work of art, the primary work of art, that points upwards, like a Gothic spire. That is the second dimension: up. The art points up to the Artist. Everything in nature is an incarnation of an idea in the mind of God.

Nature always coincides with its divine idea. Humans alone, having free choice, can fall away from it, can be what God does not know: "Depart from me, I never knew you." When we choose to coincide with our divine idea, we are God's masterpiece.

These first two dimensions of everything are like the two bars of a cross: horizontal and vertical, material and spiritual, natural and supernatural, secular and sacred, this-worldly and other-worldly, human and divine. The third dimension is *depth*. What we see with our bodies is one dimension, and what we see with our bodies-and-minds is two dimensions, but reality also has a third dimension, which neither body nor mind can see, and that is depth. Everything, especially every person, is *more*, is *deeper*, than we can see. Everything is a sea, an abyss, a deep. The most boring person you ever met is a potential god or goddess, far greater than the entire universe—or else an unimaginably hellish horror. Everything is more than it seems. We see only the scrim on the stage, the wave's first line on the beach, the epidermis of the body.

The third dimension, depth, is like a more real kind of space that transcends space. The fourth dimension, *eternity*, is like a more real kind of time that transcends time. Everything has an eternal dimension even if it is temporal, because everything real is real only because God knows it into existence, and since God is eternal, so is His knowledge; therefore, all that is real is eternal in God's mind.

A remote analogy of this happens in human memory: that kitten that died years ago still lives in your memory. You give it a second life there. For how long? For as long as you live. If your soul and your mind (not your *brain*) is immortal, so is that kitten—not in itself but in you. You are the world's God and God's world. Nothing is lost if it is loved, for if it is loved, it is remembered, and if it is remembered, it transcends time.

Only in time is anything lost. In a novel, the characters grow old and die; youth, happiness, and life are lost. But not in the novelist's mind and love! Well, life is like a novel and God is the author, so that the novel exists not only in itself (in the first three dimensions) but also in the mind of the Maker. That is its fourth, eternal dimension.

Perhaps these are the four dimensions St. Paul meant in Ephesians 3:18. That verse at least tells you what they are the dimensions *of*. What? Read it.

62. "Religion"

There is no such thing as "being religious" or "being spiritual." There is truth and there is falsehood. There is good and there is evil. There is beauty and there is ugliness. There is life and there is death. But there is not "spirituality" and "materiality," or "the sacred" and "the secular." Those are artificial abstractions, man-made, mind-made distinctions. The others are not. They are the big ones.

Why then are there special "religious" actions: liturgy? And special "religious" words: creeds? And special "religious" times: Sabbaths? And special "religious" places: churches? They are reminders of what is real always and everywhere. They are not vacations from reality, like oases in the desert. All life is liturgy. All words are creeds. All times are Sabbaths. All places are churches. But we all have attention deficit disorder; we are forgetful. And unless we see God in special places and times, we will forget to see Him in any place and time.

Nothing registers on our consciousness as a purely abstract universal truth unless it has a connection to a concrete particular. That is why God had to pick out particular prophets, form a particular "chosen people," and incarnate Himself in one particular man: one man, not all men and not "mankind." And why He had to found one particular, visible, concrete Church.

Religion is like breathing, and God is like air. Air really exists, and we really do need it, so breathing is sanity, breathing is living in reality. No one thinks breathing is weird or fanatical. But religion is to the soul what breathing is to the body. For God is certainly as real as air, as omnipresent, and as needed.

63. Nevers

Never turn your back on the ocean.

Never take the queen's knight's pawn with your queen.

Never give another driver the bird.

Never eat a sandwich with mayo in the summer if someone else made it.

Never carry fishing rods around without fixing the hooks.

Never shave in a hurry.

Never regret being hoodwinked by your love. It does you no harm to be Charlie Brown trying to kick the football, but it does do you harm to be Lucy holding it. It does you no harm to believe the Red Sox can perform another miracle. They will break your heart, of course, but it's better to have a broken heart than no heart or an unbreakable one.

The whole world is the Red Sox. They let us down and make us wise, and every once in a while they don't.

64. Work and Play

Here's some very simple stuff.

Time is life: "lifetime." That's why time management is important for life.

Rule #1 of time management: first work, then play. Do the stuff you hate to do and have to do first. This gives you six advantages:

1. Your work won't be hurried. You won't think, "I've only got one hour left. I played too long."
2. Your work won't be dogged by resentment at not being able to play anymore.
3. Your work will be more proactive and less reactive, for you have *chosen* to finish it ahead of schedule.
4. Your play won't be dogged by the unconscious worry that you won't finish your work. It's more fun to play when you're free from worry and when you know your work is done.

5. Your play will feel like your just reward to yourself. It won't feel guilty.
6. You will confront and meet your obligations instead of escaping them.

There are other rules too, and they're all obvious, e.g., make doable lists, for two reasons: so that you don't forget and lacerate yourself for forgetting, and so that you feel good about yourself for accomplishing specific things.

65. Dying Is Beginning

This one should be folded away and read when you get old.

When do you get old? When you feel: "I'm getting old."

Beginnings are always full of hope and, therefore, happiness. We have plenty of smiles and energy for beginnings.

Endings are the opposite, unless they are the endings of bad things. Endings are sad. The end of summer means no more beach days. The end of the World Series means no more baseball. So what about the end of life?

Death is the end of life (in this world) but also the beginning of life (in the next). So you can see it either way, like the glass of water that's either half empty or half full.

When we look at death as the end, we are naturally and rightly sad, whether our life was good or bad. If it was bad, we are sad with regret at what it wasn't. If it was good, we are sad with regret that it no more is what it was.

But when we look at death as the beginning (which is just as true), we are happy children again, on the shore of God's great sea, playing in His waves.

God wrote the story of human life as a serial thriller. This is only the first installment, and it ends with a dramatic flourish (death is always dramatic) and the promise "to be continued."

What makes death hopeful? Death means meeting God. Why do we feel happy and hopeful about meeting God? There are only two possible reasons. Either we are fools and know neither how holy God is nor how unholy we are, or else we know Christ.

If we are fools, we think either that God is very much like us, or that we are very much like God. We think that God is a compromiser and coward like us, or else we think that we are holy, perfect, and saintly like God.

If we are not fools, we are wise. What is the beginning of wisdom? "The fear of the Lord is the beginning of wisdom," according to His own instruction manual—but not according to most of ours. So which of the two do you honestly think is more likely to be accurate?

But fear (awe) is only the beginning of wisdom, not the end. Love is the end.

What love? God's. Our love is far too weak to be "the end (consummation) of wisdom." That's our reason for hope: His love, not ours. Christ, not Christians. God's grace, not our works. Mercy, not justice. Only fools hope for justice when they die.

God's love has a name, a face, and a cross. He put His money where His mouth is!

66. Why You Exist

By "you" here I don't mean six or seven billion human beings but you, my four absolutely unique individual children. I think you should know why you exist. I'd be a robber if I didn't give you that information.

You exist because your mother and I said "yes" to God many years ago. We said to God, "Be God. Do your thing. Create. Give yourself the children You want. We want them, too. Use us as your instruments. We will not block your way."

And when we said that to God, God said to us, "I will create them, and you will procreate them. I will love them into existence and I will use your two lovings to do that. I will make a John, a Jenny, a Katherine, and an Elizabeth, and I will also make two others whom I will take straight to Heaven before they can be born into your world, so that you will indeed have the six children you dreamed of and asked me for, but in a better way than you thought. But you will not and cannot see how my way was better than yours, as long as you are in the land of shadows. You just have to trust me."

Whatever children you have, do to them what I do to you: tell them why they exist. It's because you let God have His way. Because whenever we do that, great things happen: like you.

67. Prayers for Children

Without prayer there is no religion, just as without communication there is no friendship.

God gave us just one prayer with His own mouth: "the Lord's Prayer." He knows what He's doing, so this must be the perfect prayer. He told us His e-mail address, so if we really want to contact Him, we'll use it.

But little children don't understand the old words.

That's not so bad. The words are high and holy words, and they form the unconscious even when they don't register on the conscious.

But we need a conscious understanding, too. So here is a simple version for children to memorize or to put on a card and use each day, first thing in the morning and last thing at night. The habit of saying at least one little prayer every day is half the battle.

Our Father in Heaven,
Your name be praised!
Your Kingdom come!
Your will be done
On earth as it is in Heaven!
Give us today
Our needs for today.
And forgive us our sins
As we forgive others.
And keep us from harm
And from doing harm.
For you are the Lord of all.

68. K.I.S.S. (Keep It Simple, Stupid!)

"Life is so complicated."

No, it isn't. We make it complicated. Cars and computers and codes are complicated. Birds and bees and beaches aren't complicated. Life is wonderfully simple:

There is good, and there is evil. Love goodness.

There is truth, and there is falsehood. Love truth.

There is beauty, and there is ugliness. Love beauty.

There is life, and there is death. Love life.

There is love, and there is hate. Love love, and hate hate.

There is honesty, and there is dishonesty. Love honesty.

And then you will be deeply happy, and you will know that you have chosen rightly, and that life does not have to be complicated.

But you will know that only if you do it.

69. Therapy for Fear

When you feel afraid, look at the very first thing you see, right there in front of you: some small thing like a stone or a finger or a bug. Look at it, don't just think about looking at it. Really look. Take time. Take a whole minute.

And listen. You might hear something in it or behind it whispering some big secret to your big secret mind, some secret of which it is one of the billions of messengers, the secret of a beauty bigger than the universe, of which everything is a tiny part, including this little thing right in front of you.

Now this thing you are afraid of, this, too, is a little thing. And so are you.

God loves little things and takes care of them. Sparrows, hairs from your head.

He is bigger. He is stronger.

70. Slow Down

Doing one thing or a few things well, by slowing down and giving all your attention to them, is much more satisfying than "octopussing." "Octopussing" is a verb. It means trying to do eight things at once to try to save time. You can do that—only if you are an octopus.

Why do we "octopus"? Because we think the more things we do at once, the closer we are to being in all places, not just one. But only God is in all places. It's no fun trying to be God.

Why do we rush? Because we think the faster we move, the closer we are to being in all places at the same time. But only God moves fast enough to be in all places at the same time. It's no fun trying to be God.

Be yourself instead. "Be yourself" entails "stop rushing." There are roses to be smelled. Why do you think God put them here? For the angels? Angels have no noses.

71. "Be Good." "Why?"

That's the ultimate question in ethics. Nietzsche dared to ask it, and gave no answer. In fact, he said that it's bad to be good and good to be bad.

God gave us an answer though. "You must be holy because I, the Lord your God, am holy."

God has a habit of answering questions we never asked, so that we learn to ask them. For instance, creation is His answer to the question: Why does anything exist rather than nothing? Only those who got the answer ever asked the question: Jews and Christians, but not Greeks and Romans.

Being holy like God is not starry-eyed idealism. It's just the opposite: pure realism. God is the touchstone of realness. The reason we must be good is because we must be real.

What other answer will do? "Be good because it will make you happy"? But being good can't make you happy if it isn't real, if ultimate reality isn't God or if God isn't good. For you can't be really happy without being real.

How about "be good to others because then others will be good to you"? But they won't! In fact, if you are very good to them, they will hate you even more and even crucify you, because they can't stand being wrong where you're right. People will forgive you for being wrong, but they'll never forgive you for being right. Haven't you read the lives of the saints? Don't you know history? Ever hear of martyrs?

How about "be good to others because that's the way to build justice, fairness, equality, democracy, civilization, community, rights, and respect. . . . "? OK, but what do you say to a Nietzsche who dares to say that he doesn't give a damn about those things? All you can say is, "I have different preferences than you do." And he says to you, "I know you do. And I spit on your preferences." What do you do then? Spit back?

If you say, "But you are unjust and irrational," he will reply, "Indeed I am. So what? Why do you impose your values on me? Why do you judge me?"

And if you say that justice (and respect and all those other things) is the reason for being good, then you can't say that you should be just because it's good, because you've just said that you should be good because it's just. You're arguing in a circle. You have to come to a point. The point is God.

What happens when a circle meets a point? Make a balloon meet a pin and you will see.

72. Simple Things

What are simple things? Things that are one, not divided. Things that are not composed and, therefore, can't be decomposed. Things that are authentic and can't be debunked. (Only bunk can be debunked.) Things that are pure, not polluted.

Simple things are the most beautiful things and, therefore, the things that fascinate us and don't bore us. Things like fire, the color purple, a cat, and a wave. Simple things have no interstices, holes, or joints. You can't take them apart. You can't take a cat apart as you can take a toy apart.

We simply need simple things. We need them absolutely. We need complex things too, but only relatively, not absolutely. We need complex things to serve simple things, not to be served by them. Toys are for cats, not cats for toys. Complex things are relative; simple things are absolute. The number 1 is not relative to 1/3, but 1/3 is relative to 1. It is 1 made complex by the addition of "divide by 3."

God is simple, not complex. He is not divided or divisible. The Father, the Son, and the Spirit are not three parts of God. God has no parts. He is not one by number, like one set of triplets, or one triplet. He is one by love. ("God *is* love.") His 3 *is* 1 and His 1 *is* 3. He is so one that He is the oneness even of oneness and threeness.

Simple things make us happy because they take us beyond time. They just *smell* eternal. They are impervious to progress and, therefore, to regress. They never appear in newspaper headlines. When did you last see the news that a boy played with a stick and a stone by the river?

Love is the simplest thing of all, and *agape,* the love that is simple, self-forgetful goodwill, is the simplest love of all. That's why God is infinitely simple. Much too simple for us complex creatures to understand.

73. Understanding

The very first philosophical discovery I ever made, the first original bit of wisdom I ever discovered, somewhere around the age of eight, I think, was this: "A little understanding is better than a lot of long-suffering." The occasion for this discovery was some sort of altercation I was having with my mother based on what I thought was her long-suffering failure to understand me.

I wish I had taken my own advice much more with my own family, because we all want to be understood, not tolerated. One of the most frustrating words to hear is "whatever." It's a cheap substitute for understanding. No, not even a substitute, but a repudiation, a refusal to understand. It's "toleration." How wimpy and cop-outish of our culture to rank mere toleration so high, or to be satisfied with that! It's better than intolerance, of course, but almost every other virtue is better than it.

Is there a secret to understanding? To understanding any-thing, even persons? Yes. This: understanding comes only from deliberate, willed effort. Attention is an act of the mind only because it is commanded by the will.

74. If

If spouses were as polite to each other as they are to strangers . . .

If we were as good to each other as our own dogs are to each other . . .

If we were as good to each other as we are to our dogs . . .

If we were as careful for our souls as we are for our bodies . . .

If we were as careful for our bodies as we are for our money

 . . . why, then, we would be almost sane.

75. Life Is a Fish Fry

And all the while God waits patiently, with a cosmic sense of humor, and carefully fries His small fish (us), turning them over minimally until they are done, not rushing them or breaking them or overspicing them, knowing just how much attention and pain we need to soften us up. And then, after what seems to us a lot of wasted time and suffering, we emerge from the frying pan of purgatory and we find that He has made us able to not only endure but to enjoy our limitations and imperfections, those of others, and those of the earth; and then we will understand that if it were not for those limits, against which we have bumped repeatedly and resentfully, at the cost of much skin and blood from our egos—were it not for those limits, our identities could not have been sculpted and our souls would be like wet spaghetti.

God does this to us despite our spittings and squirmings in the pan, and He does it through other people, who are the very spatulas by which He turns us around in His frying pan. And we are His spatulas for "frying" others. How humbling: "What are you good for?"

"Being a spatula."

"What does that mean?"

"It means turning others over like fish in the pan even when they want to be left alone."

"What do you mean, turning them over? Deliberately?"

"No, not usually; just being myself."

"Oh, but that's a good thing: to be yourself."

"It doesn't seem so good to the fish."

"I don't understand. You mean you think your very being yourself pisses people off?"

"Of course! We are fish, not pieces of a jigsaw puzzle. We don't fit. Our protuberances bump the protuberances of the other fish. And that's precious."

"Precious? You said it pisses people off. How can it be precious? I don't understand."

"You're not married, are you?"

We become gemstones only on the grinding wheel.

76. How to Get Peace and Social Justice

Some say the road to peace is justice. Some say the road to justice is peace. I say the only way to justice, between nations in the world or between individuals in families, is to stop demanding justice and seek forgiveness instead. Seek it and also give it. It's hard to get from injustice to justice in places like Palestine, but it's always possible to get to forgiveness. For we can't get to justice just by choosing it, but we can get to forgiveness just by choosing it. Warring Israelis and Palestinians will never stop accusing each other of injustices, because they are both right. Each side keeps committing injustices against the other. That's the basic fact, even if one side is more unjust than the other, and even if one "started it." They will never find a mutually acceptable justice. Neither will any pair of feuding spouses, friends, or nations. The more we demand justice, the more we demand our rights, the harder it will be to achieve them, except by force. The only road to peace is radical forgiveness. Jesus didn't talk about justice, He talked about forgiveness.

77. Peace

But unless you are already at peace with yourself, you can't practice the road to peace that is forgiveness. Instead, you will project the war you have with yourself out onto the other.

Thomas Merton says we are not at peace with each other because we are not at peace with ourselves, and we are not at peace with ourselves because we are not at peace with God. That's the whole problem of conflict in two sentences.

Why do you have to bring God into it? I don't bring God into it; He *is* in it, in the very center of it, because He touches us at the very center of the self, where we are subject, not object, "I," not "he" or "she." Augustine calls Him "the One who is more intimately present to me than I am to myself." *That's* why Merton was right.

78. Why We Need Unhappiness

Your muscles get stronger only by exercise, and exercise means meeting resistance, surfaces that oppose them. Boxers need sparring partners to train with. Our souls are boxers, too, and need hard times to spar with. The muscles of the soul are courage and character. They get strong only through struggle and pain. In fact, they get strong only with some defeats, because strength of soul means wisdom, and wisdom comes from suffering. We learn the most from our mistakes.

You can't be deeply happy unless you have a deep, strong soul. You can't have a deep, strong soul unless you have suffered deep unhappiness. Therefore you can't be deeply happy without ever being deeply unhappy.

Knowing this doesn't take away unhappiness. If it did, it would take away happiness, too.

Wisdom is not a drug for pain. But it gets you out of bed, up and moving, instead of giving up, copping out, or moaning.

79. Why Honesty Is the Most Important Virtue

Because it's the beginning. It's not the end, the highest thing. Love is the end. But honesty is the beginning because honesty means the demand for truth, and love needs truth because it needs to be not just some love but true love.

Both honesty and its opposite, dishonesty, are unlimited. They are not like a mountain and a valley but like the day and the night: they can be spread over *everything*.

The daylight of honesty chases away all darkness, cleans out all hidden dirt. And the dark night of dishonesty hides everything, beautiful things as well as ugly things.

Better to be an honest troublemaker, atheist, and pessimist than a dishonest helper, believer, and optimist. For your honesty, like the rising sun, will eventually expose and reveal those dark things and they will die in the light like Dracula. But your dishonesty will gradually infect all the good things and suck their lifeblood from them and turn them into the walking dead. There will be a hidden fear of exposure, an evasion, a distrust, a *shuffling*, that will permeate your whole life like a fog.

We are not designed for darkness, we are designed for light. Our homeland is the country of the bright angels, and we must learn to endure more and more light as we get closer to home.

80. The Profoundest Wisdom

At the summit of the mountain of wisdom is a little hobbit hut.

"I love you" is something even the severely retarded can say with their eyes. Yet it is impossible for the world's greatest sage to say anything more profound.

It is the simplest sentence of all because it is the closest to God's speech. What God keeps saying to us in every baby, every wave, every raindrop, snowfall, star, and rose, over and over again, with infinite patience, until we finally get it, is: "I love you. I love you. I love you."

"I love you" were my father's last words to me. I will make them my last words to you.

81. Last Resort

Sometimes the only possible solution to a problem that has you on the verge of self-inflicted baldness or holes in the wall is the following prescription:

1. ten deep breaths
2. a hot bath
3. one large glass of good wine
4. and a good night's sleep

After patience, philosophy, and prayer all seem to fail, try listening to your body.

82. Gratitude

When we realize that "everything is a grace," beginning with our very existence and culminating with our salvation, we wish we could give God something in return. But what? He is perfect and needs nothing.

I have three answers.

1. He needs nothing but He wants something. He wants it so much that He went to unimaginable trouble to get it. (Watch Mel Gibson's movie again.) He wants our trust and our love. It's the one thing God cannot give Himself, because He is not us.

2. He gave us something to give to Him, like a rich parent giving his kids some of his own money to buy him Christmas presents. In fact, He gave us something to give Him that is worth more than the entire created universe, even including all its human beings and angels. He gave us Himself in Jesus. The Mass is our offering of that perfect gift, the only perfect gift, to God,

in thanksgiving for the same gift to us. "Eucharist" *means* "thanksgiving."

3. We can even bail God out of a jam, a dilemma. His dilemma is this: Love always wants the beloved both to *be* good and to *feel* good (i.e., happy). To make us to be happy, God often has to make us feel unhappy, because we forget Him when we are happy and comfortable, and turn to Him only when we are not.

God doesn't like it when His kids suffer, any more than we do. But He *has* to let us suffer because we'd forget Him if we didn't, and then we'd suffer more. So if we remember Him by gratitude when things go well, He won't have to plunge us into shock to wake us up, and then both He and we would be much happier.

We really can make God happy by being grateful. We can really do that something for Him, because even though He is eternal, He is love, and love cares. Love is not a cold fish.

We can't blackmail Him, we can't make Him sad, like a small, spoiled child holding his breath until his face turns blue to get his mother upset. But though we can't make Him unhappy, we can make Him happy. His happiness is already infinite, but we can add to it, we can add to infinity. You can't subtract anything from infinity, but you can add to it. You can infinitely add to it.

83. Three Stupid Thoughts

Here are three things people think about too much. The three thoughts are not stupid in themselves—in fact, all three are quite profound—but we usually think about them too much, and that is stupid because all three are medicines, not foods, and we usually think of them as foods. It's stupid to think of medicines as often as we think of foods.

The first is *freedom*. The wise seldom speak of freedom because the wise are those who love, and lovers do not speak of freedom. Lovers want to be bound, not free. They don't seek freedom because they are already free if they are lovers.

The second is *rights*. The wise seldom speak of rights for the same reason: lovers don't ask for their rights, they ask for their beloved. They do think about their beloved's rights, but only when they are threatened.

Even the bigger notion of *right* rather than *rights*—being right, being in the right—is not as great as we think, at least when it comes to relationships. Being wrong is sometimes far less threatening to a relationship than being right. People will forgive you for being wrong, but not for being right.

They will understand you and accept you quite easily when you are wrong, but not nearly so easily when you are right. Sometimes, "no good deed goes unpunished." This is because when you are bad, they feel good about themselves, since they feel better than you, but when you are good, they feel bad about themselves, since you are better than them.

The solution is not to be bad, and to be wrong, but to stop *thinking* about being right or even about being good, just *do* it.

The third idea we think about too much is *myself*. Self-consciousness makes us human, of course, but it also messes us up. We usually do it exactly when we shouldn't: when we're good and not when we're bad. Self-consciousness interrupts whatever we're doing, so we should use it to interrupt the bad, not the good. Instead, we think: "Oh, what a good person I am being now!"—and that stops the goodness. We should think: "Oh, what an ass I am being now!"—and that will stop the asininity.

We need periodic self-checks, of course, at how we're doing a job, but when it comes to the job of life, we have a dilemma when we judge ourselves. Here is the dilemma and the way out of it:

The dilemma is really a trilemma. Possibility #1 is giving yourself a high grade: I'm doing really well, I'm a really good person. In other words, I'm God's gift to the rest of you. I'm a pharisee, and I'm proud of myself and of my humility.

Possibility #2 is giving yourself a low grade: I'm a failure, I stink, I'm bad. We all know how *that* thought messes you up. One time in a thousand it may have the shock power to lead to honest repentance and reform, but 999 times in 1,000 it leads to self-deceptive cover-ups like addictions, and taking out your self-hate on others. The thought "I'm worse than you" protects itself by words and behaviors that say "You're worse than me."

Possibility #3 is giving yourself a mediocre grade, neither hot nor cold but lukewarm, wishy-washy. That can be even worse than the other two in a way, because it makes you like a car with no fuel, no passion, going nowhere.

The solution to the trilemma is simple: let God judge you and others. Don't judge. Just do your job, forget yourself. God gave us selves to see other selves with, just as He gave us eyes to see other eyes with. Ingrown eyeballs are as ugly and painful as ingrown toenails. Don't be a spiritual hypochondriac.

84. How to Deal with Difficult People

What to do when someone bad-mouths you?
Praise them.
What to do when someone hurts you?
Help them.
What to do when someone rejects you?
Accept them.
They bad-mouth, hurt, and reject because they are weak.
You should praise, help, and accept because you are strong.

And above all, remember that to everyone else who reads this, the "difficult people" includes you.

85. All Fathers
Fail but One

I just read this in Tolkien's letters to his grown children: "I live in anxiety concerning my children, who in this harder, crueler, and more mocking world into which I have survived must suffer more assaults than I have. . . . I have brought you all up ill and talked to you too little. . . . I failed as a father. Now I pray for you all, unceasingly, that the Healer shall heal my defects."

Joseph Pearce, Tolkien's biographer, comments: "One cannot help but feel that Tolkien was being unduly harsh in seeing himself as a failure as a father. Whatever shortcomings he exhibited must be countered by the mitigating pleas of those who remembered him as a loving and conscientious parent."

Pearce was still young when he wrote that. When he gets as old as Tolkien was when he wrote his letter, he will understand, and perhaps write one like it to his children. What parents can look back and be satisfied with their own efforts? Only shallow and materialistic fools. ("My kids never lacked any toy the other kids had!")

Good parents are never satisfied with their efforts to love and understand their kids, but they are satisfied with their kids. How can we be satisfied with the results of our efforts but not with our efforts? Because the good in our kids now is due 1% to us, 2% to them, and 97% to God's grace.

There is only one perfect Father. And even His kids mess up. All of them.

86. The Best Gift to Your Kids

When you become a daddy, the very best thing you can do for your kids is this: love mommy.

When you become a mommy, the very best thing you can do for your kids is this: love daddy.

Make the footsteps right and beautiful, the footsteps that others will walk in.

87. One-Word Advice
for Marriage

The most frequent complaint troubled couples bring to marriage counselors is: "We don't love each other any more." The answer to it is a single word: "Do."

Love doesn't happen, like rain. You do it.

But isn't love a feeling? No. That's like saying a flower is a smell.

88. Two Philosophies
of Life

Philosophy #1: Life sucks, people suck, and if one morning you wake up to find everything looking beautiful and people loving each other, you're either dreaming or dead.

Logic can prove that life is sad. For life is either sad or happy, and if life is sad, well, then, it's sad; and if it's happy, that's even sadder, because it has to end.

Philosophy #2: Life is beautiful, and people do love each other, and if one day you find that everything sucks, you're in a bad dream.

Logic can prove that life is happy. For life is either happy or sad, and if life is happy, well, then, it's happy; and if it's sad, then it's happy, too, because the sadness has to end.

Your choice. Logic is on your side either way.

89. Holy Shit

It's not a curse, it's an insight: shit is holy.

Because everything God makes is holy.

Because breathing out the bad air is just as holy as breathing in the good air.

Because the humblest things are the holiest.

Because the earthiest things are the most heavenly.

And because even when "shit" is a euphemism for "that hurts," it's a holy thing, too, because God uses suffering to save us. (Read the Book.)

90. Jacob's Ladder

"This is a holy place, and I knew it not," said Jacob after he saw the ladder for a moment, with its angels ascending and descending on it.

The ladder means the whole world. Every place is holy. Every place is full of angels.

It also means Jesus. He said so. It's in John's Gospel. Look it up. I won't tell you where it is so that you will have to read the whole book to find it.

91. Forgive

There hasn't been a single day of my life when I was just the true me, the person I want to be, which is the person God wants me to be.

Every day I have failed to be me to God, to myself, and to you. But I trust you will forgive me because God has forgiven me, and you don't want to disagree with God.

He's going to make me fully me in Heaven, and then I'll be able to be me to you.

Forgiveness, not achievement and success, is our hope. Endless waves of forgiveness. And afterward, waves of laughter.

92. What to Do
Ten Times a Day
to Be Happy

Premise one: We're happy when we're home, when we're where we belong, where we're designed to be.

Premise two: Our home is praise. God designed us to know Him in His works and to praise Him and enjoy Him there. That's why He gave us His works, the universe: to sing from. It's our first hymn book.

The conclusion is obvious. We are happy when we sing His praises.

Here's how to look at the hymn book. At least ten times each day do something that takes only about five seconds. First, just take one deep breath. (There, that wasn't so hard, now, was it?) That alone can be radical healing for workaholics. Pause for the five seconds it takes you to take that one breath, and praise God for one little thing you notice: the color of the sky, or your skin, or the curve of wood in the chair you're sitting on or the human craft that shaped it, or the wipeout of the dinosaurs that allowed your body to evolve, or your ability to see, hear, feel, create, understand and to make others understand—or for the sheer existence of anything, everything, of a single grain of sand. (Because nothing *had* to exist. Everything is a gift.) Just thank Him for one new thing every hour for ten hours every day. That takes 5 x 10 = 50 seconds. Less than one minute. And yet I guarantee that it will make you a lot happier and less harried, hassled, angry, fearful, worried, and more aware of real things instead, things you've seen a million times but never noticed.

You see, this is not an *idea* or a *philosophy* that you can disagree with. It's just being real, noticing reality. It's not a trick you play on yourself. Just the opposite: ordinary worry-consciousness is the trick we play on ourselves. This is a way out of the trick into realism.

And it will make you happier. Have you got a problem with that? Gratitude always makes you happy. Count your blessings—literally—and the number will astound you.

"But I don't feel like doing that most of the time." Right. That's exactly why you need to do it, and when you need to do it most: when you feel like doing it least.

It's better than pills. It's like magic. And all it costs is a minute a day.

It's a long-range investment. If you invested one dollar a day at compound interest from age ten, you'd be a millionaire by the time you're seventy. Invest one minute a day in gratitude and you'll be a happier, wiser, better person in the end. And this is a better investment because unlike money, you can take it with you.

The only time you can't do it is when you're sneezing. That's why someone else does it for you then: "God bless you." Be sure you remember to say that for them, too. Remember me every time someone sneezes.

93. What Not to Do Ten Times a Day

In addition to doing the exercise above ten times a day, here is one to *stop* doing ten times a day or more: noticing all the shit and keeping it in your mind. That's like not flushing the toilet. We can't always change the shit, but we can always change our mind. "Shit happens," but why keep sniffing it?

"Shit" doesn't mean your responsibilities. The baby's eyes are red: does she have a cold? Your friend is depressed: why? You have a recurrent pain: get it looked at. By "the shit," I mean things like insults, taxes, wrinkles.

94. Ten Sentences Nobody Ever Uttered on His Deathbed

1. "I wish I had spent more time at the office and less with my family."
2. "I wish I had spent more time being selfish."
3. "I wish I hadn't wasted all that time praying."
4. "I wish I had spent more time making money."
5. "I wish I had spent more time seeking knowledge and less time seeking wisdom."
6. "I wish I had spent more time worrying about justice and less about compassion."
7. "I wish I had spent more time thinking about my rights and less about others'."
8. "I wish I had spent more time thinking about freedom and autonomy and less about love and harmony."
9. "I wish I had spent more time thinking about better sanitation, transportation, and economics and less about that escapist fantasy called Heaven."
10. "How godlike man is!"

95. Priorities

God is #1, family is #2, and everything else is, at best, merely a matter of life or death.

96. Eat the Fruits
in the Toy Box

Each day God brings a thousand good things into our lives that we don't notice. But when He allows one bad thing, it fills our mind's whole horizon.

God lets us do an infinity of good things. Only ten are forbidden. But we want the few forbidden fruits that are poisonous when there are unlimited fruits that aren't poisonous in the big toy box called nature that God made for us to play in.

He put some of His own mysterious magnetism into everything in that toy box. That's why a little kid gets bored with a video game quicker than with a ball and a bat, or the ocean. And that's why we love sunlight, trees, beaches, snow, foods, and animals.

97. The Burning I

Prayer is not only conversation, it is transformation. It is not only light, it is fire. And the closer you get to Him, the hotter the fire gets. Words begin to melt. The first word that melts in His presence is the word "I." That is *His* unique name. The closer you get to Him, the harder it is to begin a sentence with "I." It melts in the fire of "thou."

98. Mystic to the Max: A Lesson in Comparative Religions

Do you want to be a mystic?

Why?

Because they know God the most.

No they don't. You already know God better than Buddha ever did.

Why?

Because you know Jesus. A Christian is a mystic to the max, because "he who has seen me, has seen the Father."

Buddha never saw the Father. And even those who, unlike Buddha, spoke profoundly of God (and called Him "Brahman," "Allah," or "Tao") never dreamed of calling Him "Father."

99. You Wanna be a Saint?

Who, me? Moi? You gotta be kidding.

Was Jesus kidding?

No, but that's for monks and mystics, not for schmucks and schlemiels like me.

Didn't you read the Gospels? Jesus never talked to monks or mystics, only to schmucks and schlemiels, starting with the twelve apostles.

Well, then, I'll just be a good egg.

You can't just be a good egg. If you don't hatch, you will become a bad egg.

What is it to hatch?

To become a saint.

I'm not good enough to become a saint.

What a silly excuse! You want to wait until you're saintly before you start being saintly?

I'm not perfect enough to be perfect.

Good. That's step 1 in becoming a saint: honesty, realism and humility. Now go on to step 2.

He doesn't accept any excuses?

Nope.

Why not?

Because all your excuses for not doing it are worse than ridiculous.

What do you mean, "worse than ridiculous?"

"Ridiculous" is just "naturally stupid," "humanly stupid." Our excuses for not being saints, for not being very good and, therefore, very happy, are so bad that they must come from something other than our own laziness.

What do you mean? From where?

Figure it out: where are all the saints going to live?

Heaven.

So ask yourself: Who's trying to keep you from that?

Oops.

We're not in a smorgasbord restaurant with Heaven as one option. We're on a battlefield with Heaven as one army.

"Be a saint" is not a human *option*, it's a divine *order* from General God.

100. "Joy in Suffering"—Impossible?

I do not wish you suffering, I wish you joy. But I wish you also the strange but beautiful sweetness of joy in suffering.

It can come only from a suffering that comes from love and trust, a suffering that you know is God's will for you and that you therefore accept in the simple trust that (1) He loves you and therefore wishes only your deepest joy, (2) that He knows exactly what He's doing and exactly what you need, and (3) that He is in control of every atom in the universe He created. If any one of those three things isn't true, then there is no God, only "the force," which does not love you, or Zeus, who's stupid, or Apollo, who's weak.

When you know this, and when you turn to what you know instead of ignoring it, God will sometimes give you the grace of a supernatural joy, a joy that seems to be irrational, a joy without a cause, an utterly unexpected and unexplainable gift. We can't control it, we can't understand it, and we can't even desire it. But we can trust Him and be ready if He gives it.

101. Nature and Grace

St. Theresa said on her deathbed, "everything is grace." That's true. But that doesn't mean that nothing is nature. Nature is the nature of grace. Nature is grace's body.

And grace perfects nature. So the more grace, the more nature.

This is especially true of free will. When we freely choose something good, that's really God's grace, and that's really our freedom. The two are not rivals, like two swords, but like the two edges of a single sword.

Therefore thank God not only when something good comes *to* you without your choice, but also when something good comes *from* you by your choice, because it's also coming from Him if it's good.

102. Anorexia of the Soul

We all have it. God is the food our souls are designed to eat, and when we do, we put on weight, muscle, and power; when we don't, we creak, break, and bump into things.

That's why St. Paul always expresses *joy* at the faith of the people he writes his epistles to, like a father who loves his children and knows the joylessness that comes from not eating God, and the joy that comes from eating God, the God who made Himself into our food. The father feels the children's joys and sorrows as his own. His joy is like the "Aaaah!" that comes out of you spontaneously when you see your kids get well after being sick and like the "Aaaah!" that comes out of you when you eat a delicious meal.

103. Bumpers and Bleeders versus Noodles and Skeletons

Love is tough by its essential nature, not by the addition of some foreign substance. Love is a rock, not a noodle.

Many people are noodles and think that adding spicy sauce will cover up their limp souls. It will, but only to the taste, not to the feel or the digestion.

Love is also tender by its essential nature, not by the addition of some foreign substance like meat tenderizer. Love is not a bony skeleton anymore than it is a boneless skin.

Many people are skeletons and think that wearing soft clothes will cover their hard, brittle souls. It will, but only to gullible fools.

Being a noodle is easy and attractive because that way you can go through life without bumping into anybody. Being a skeleton is easy and attractive because that way you can go through life without bleeding. But real people are bumpers and bleeders.

104. How to Be Wiser, Happier, and Better in Seven Minutes

If you're not interested in these three products, don't read this. If you are in the market for them but skeptical about getting them in seven minutes, read on.

The answer is three words: count your blessings. It's so simple it's embarrassing.

I mean this literally. Just thank God for seven specific blessings. Don't ask Him for anything, just thank Him.

If you want a structure, here is one: tell God you are grateful for the following seven specific things. (They can be small things; small things are best because we don't usually notice them.)

1. one specific, concrete thing in the world
2. one specific, concrete thing in your life
3. one specific event in the world
4. one specific event in your life

5. one specific person in the world
6. one specific person in your life
7. one attribute, aspect, or deed of God Himself

Results guaranteed.

105. God Is a Comedian

Don't be more serious than God. God invented dog farts. God designed your body's plumbing system. God designed an ostrich. If He didn't do it, He permitted a drunken angel to do it.

Empirical facts can add significantly to the meaning of "being godlike."

106. A Realistic Thought Experiment

Nothing is more real or more certain than that someday you will die.

So no thought experiment is more realistic than this one: do and say today what you would want to do or say on the last day of your life.

For today may well be that day. Someday certainly will.

And whatever you would *not* want to do or say on the last day of your life, don't do or say that today. For exactly the same reason.

Practice! (How to live, in one word.)

107. Hokiness

We're deterred from much good by fear of being hokey, fear of embarrassment. We'd rather be thought to be almost anything rather than be thought hokey, square, uncool, unhip, naïve, sentimental, or whatever the latest teenage embarrassment word is.

The fear comes from what others may think. But others are not going to stay with us forever, only God is. Let's be realistic! And, therefore, let's be sentimental or hokey or square sometimes. God is. He invented cows as well as lions.

108. Blessed Mess

History is full of discarded scientific theories. Almost all of them were too neat. The real universe has always proved to be messier, more mysterious and surprising than our dreams.

And that tells you something about its Creator and ours and, therefore, us.

Living things delight us because of their moreness, their messiness. We love trees more than the neat houses we make out of them, though we don't know why. We love real animals more than mechanical animals, and we do know why.

Eighteenth-century Europeans liked to confine nature in perfectly geometrical formal gardens. Thirteenth-century Europeans liked to confine the universe to perfectly geometrical concentric spheres, with the earth right smack in the center. Wrong, wrong. Even the earth isn't quite geometrical: it's not a sphere but a pancake, about 8 miles fatter through the equator than through the poles. Your own body looks isomorphic but it isn't; your heart is a little bit to one side. God is "tricksy," as Gollum would say.

We expect Him to be either nothing (atheism) or a vague everything (pantheism), or purely one (rationalism), or merely many (pagan polytheism), but He turns out to be One in three! Why? Because love has to be three: lover, beloved, and loving. To be complete is to be messy to our simplistic expectations.

He could have put a simple sign up in the Garden of Eden: "No Snakes Allowed." He could have solved all the world's problems by miracles. Instead, He designed the mystery that is our history and the mess that is our bless.

So the next time He treats you like Job, don't be scandalized by the shit pile. (The word is in the Bible: "dung heap." Do you want to *correct* it, like a prim schoolmarm?)

Ivan Karamazov called himself a "rebel." He didn't want to rebel against God but he thought he had to because he rebelled against God's world: its injustices and irrationalities and messiness: its shit. His brother Alyosha loved God *and* His world, because God did.

Be close to the earth and you will be close to the heavens.

Ivan's hope was that he still loved "the sticky little leaves."

109. A Parable about Walls

Once upon a time there was a foolish man who hated walls. When he was a baby, he kept climbing out of his crib. When he was a boy, he kept running away from home. When he was a teenager, he kept breaking all the rules. When he was an adult, he became an *artist* (which is to be distinguished from becoming an artist) because he thought that *art* (as distinct from art) was where rules were made to be broken.

He hated all walls, especially the needs, demands, and "interferences" of other people. He would talk big about "artistic and personal integrity," by which he meant infantile self-centeredness. He would pompously denounce "compromise," by which he meant discipline. Of course, he became famous. Those who knew his work called him "brilliant," "creative," and "original." Those who knew *him* called him less complimentary things.

One day he realized that the logic of his philosophy of life necessitated suicide, because the world was just too full of walls, and he thought that suicide was the only way out of the world. He thought that his "true self," like bathwater let out of a tub drain, would eventually make its destined way to the wall-free sea of being. (He was a self-styled mystic and very "spiritual," and therefore hated "organized religion" for its walls.)

When he died, the water of his being did indeed go down the drain. But when he reached the sea, he found it to be a sea of emptiness, not water. For water, too, is a wall. It has a nature, being one thing and not another, and imposed limits and conditions on all who would know it or enjoy it.

So since we all get what we want in the end, he fell forever and ever through the wall-free infinity of empty space and time that some call Hell, which is the only place without walls. For another name for walls is "the way things are," "the nature of things," and "reality."

110. Your Life: Four Images

1. If you think of your life as an investment, you will be disappointed because there will always be red ink as well as black.

   So don't even say "my glass of water is half full, not half empty," because that's *counting*. Counting saves money, but it can lose life. Life passes through its fingers.
2. If you think of your life as computer programming, you will be resentful because it will always have some hidden trick to play on you that you didn't program into it, and the total control that you expected will never be yours.
3. If you think of your life as a baseball game, that's better because all the players have fun, even the losers, and nobody loses all the time, not even the Cubs.
4. But if you think of your life as a tumble in the surf, that's best of all because that's jumping for joy and laughing even in wipe-outs.

111. "I Didn't Deserve That"

The next time something bad happens to you through no fault of your own, and you are about to complain to God, "I didn't deserve that," look at a crucifix and say those same words to Him: "I didn't deserve that." It gives you a sense of perspective.

112. "Liberal" or "Conservative"?

The Church, like the state, seems split between the "liberals" and the "conservatives," the progressives and the traditionalists. The "liberals" insist on compassion, humanism, love, outreach, service, openness, tolerance, equality, and experiment. The "conservatives" insist on dogma, truth, tradition, hierarchy, holiness, authority, and obedience. These seem to be two different spirits, almost two different religions.

The concrete solution to the division is the sacrament of confession. When you have sinned and know it, you don't *want* the priest in the confessional to sound like a "judgmental" conservative and remind you of the law, the truth, and justice. But you also don't want him to sound like a "tolerant" liberal humanist or pop psychologist. You don't want him to be "judgmental," but don't want him to be "nonjudgmental" either. You want him to say those uncompromisingly "conservative," dogmatic words, and you want the words to be absolutely, exactly, objectively, and eternally true: "By the authority given to me by Christ and His apostles, I declare to you forgiveness for all your sins in the name of the Father and of the Son and of the Holy Spirit."

You don't want him to water down or alter one word of that absolutistic, authoritarian formula. You know, at that point, that there is no way to the fullness of the Church's "liberal" end, of healing and peace and acceptance, except through the fullness of the Church's "conservative" medicine. You want the Church to be infallible and dogmatic at that point, and you want it desperately. At that point, the two things you usually call "liberal" and "conservative" show their true colors as artificial ideological abstractions.

This healing of the "liberal/conservative" dilemma comes from the confessional. So if you're a pharisee who thinks you don't need the confessional, you'll probably never get to it. There are two kinds of pharisees: very liberal ones who don't believe in a real, objective, unchangeable moral law, and very conservative ones who believe in hardly anything else. In other words, illegalists and legalists. God is a translegalist.

113. When You Fail

There will come a time when you simply fail, inexcusably, terribly. You will feel yourself standing among the shattered pieces of a beautiful work of art that you just broke. You will surprise yourself that you were that stupid. No, not just stupid, bad. Morally weak.

You will fail at something incomparably important. You will feel that *you* are a failure. You will feel no compensation. You will feel despair and hopelessness. Perhaps you know what I'm talking about; perhaps you've gone through that already.

The experience of our own faults comes as a surprise to us because our teachers no longer talk about fault, or failure, or sin. They no longer tell us about our inner Judas, about that spiteful little bastard who lives in the basement of the soul.

You will hurt the ones you love. You will lie about it. You will do something embarrassingly bad and not face up to it. You will give others excuses, because you will first give yourself excuses. (The spiteful little bastard is very good at finding them, and our sick society is very good at supplying them; they work in tandem, those two.) And if you don't have the inner toughness of spirit, the honesty and courage to confess to yourself, then you won't be able to confess to God and to those you hurt either. And then the rot will stay there inside the potato and spread until it rots your life so obviously that you can no longer deny it—or, even worse, until it rots your mind so much that you can no longer admit it.

By the way, there are two philosophies of man. One says we rot like lettuce, from outside in. The other says we rot like potatoes, from inside out. The first blames others, "society," Republicans, Democrats, UFOs, or social structures. The second says, "We have met the enemy and they are us." The theological term for that idea is "original sin." It's a dogma.

We all fail. That's why one of His sacraments is confession. No one except Jesus and His mother ever lived without sin. The choices we make between the two roads, good and evil, saint and sinner, is the second most important choice. The most important choice comes especially *after* you sin. Then the two roads are honest confession or cover-up and avoidance, light or darkness. The dark way seems easier and more comfortable. But no one has ever found peace at the end of that road, and everyone who has ever taken the other road, the uncomfortably bright one, has found exactly that.

There are problems that can be helped by words, and there are others that can't. But even then, God is God, and God is good beyond words.

When you are in trouble, remember that He is present even when you feel Him least. So is your guardian angel. I will be, too, once God has freed me from the limitations of this body. You are not alone, ever. You are loved, always.

114. Love and Pain

The best thing in life is not the thing we want the most. The best thing is to love. The thing we want the most is to be loved. The most fearsome thing is not loving, but the thing we fear the most is not being loved.

Why do we fear that the most? Because it gives us the most pain.

To love is to give your heart away into someone else's hands. To give your heart away is to be vulnerable to pain. If you give your heart away, it will certainly be broken, many times. But the only whole heart is a broken heart. Love and pain are a package deal. The only way to avoid pain is to avoid love, to give your heart to no one, to put a security system around it. It will be safe there in the freezer. But it will not beat. It will freeze. (In Dante, the lowest realm of Hell is not fire but ice.)

We give too much of our hearts to little things, like image and control, that are not worth the pain. More important, we give too little of our hearts to big things, like loving God and our families, because we unconsciously fear the pain. In making this foolish calculation, we forget one thing: that love's joy always outweighs love's pain in the end; that no sane person has ever said on his deathbed: "I shouldn't have loved so much. I shouldn't have put out so much. I should have kept my heart in the freezer." Long before that, if there is love, then there is a joy even *in* the pain of making free, willing sacrifices and freely accepting the unwilled pains. And even when that joy takes a while to come, there is always the peace that comes from knowing that you did the right thing.

115. Cheap Psychiatry

Being a Catholic can save you a lot of money. Confession is free, psychiatrists are expensive.

We have four options:

1. Be a happy, holy, well-integrated person with no big problems.
2. Mess up and deal with it. Turn back to the source. Go to confession.
3. Mess up and use psychiatrists and psychologists instead. (It doesn't have to be "instead." Good confessors will sometimes send you to psychologists, and good psychologists will sometimes send you to confessors.) That will take more time and money than confession, and it has no guarantee that it will always "work," as confession does.
4. Mess up and don't deal with it in either of the two above ways. Cover up.

The first is the cheapest but also the rarest.

The fourth is the most expensive of all in the long run, because the harm that any disease does to you, in body or soul, always increases in time.

116. The Power of Confession

We don't remember being washed as a baby, but we can see the smiles on baby's face, so we know how good it feels. And we know how good it feels to wash off the dirt, sweat, and grime after a hard, hot day. Just suppose we could do for our souls what we can do for our bodies, with no more physical effort than walking into the bathtub.

We can. The confessional is a bathtub. It's a baby changing room. Mommy Church changes our dirty diapers there.

Even more than that, the confessional is a transformer. Adam walks in and Christ walks out.

117. Minds and Mouths

The less open your mind is, the more open your mouth usually is. You gotta vent your soul somehow.

Open minds inhale; open mouths exhale. You can smell the difference between the two kinds of air.

118. Keep a Chapbook

A practical idea for you: buy a blank book (with a beautiful cover to remind you how precious this book is going to be) and copy down in it the words you've found the wisest, most helpful, and most beautiful from any and all sources, so that you don't forget them and so that you can keep coming back to them and drink their water again. This is what used to be called a chapbook. It's purely yours, purely individual, and it can be purely private, so you don't have to pretend or wear any masks.

Here are three examples of quotations I would put in mine:

1. "Man, please thy Maker and be merry/And for this world give not a cherry." (Robert Herrick)
2. "Just love your brother and drink a good glass of red wine every day." (Advice from Antonia Todde, an Italian shepherd listed by the Guinness Book of World Records as the world's oldest man, at 112.)

3. "Out of the darkness of my life, so much frustrated, I put before you the one great thing to love on earth: the Blessed Sacrament. There you will find romance, glory, honour, fidelity, and the true way of all your loves on earth . . . by . . . which alone can what you seek in your earthly relationships (love, faithfulness, joy) be maintained, and take on that complexion of reality, of eternal endurance, which every man's heart desires." (J. R. R. Tolkien, letter to his son Christopher)

119. God and Play

The morning offering offers to God "all my prayers, works, joys and sufferings of this day." The one we forget the most is the joys. We forget that the joy of play is God's gift. We separate God and play. We forget to thank Him for it, and we forget to play in front of Him. But He designed play as well as work. Though both became bent after the fall, both remain great goods.

Connecting God and play is not itself merely a matter of play; forgetting that connection is serious, for it makes our religion playless and joyless, and our joy and play irreligious.

Just as we should work and pray and suffer in God, we should play in God. Think of a wipe-out on a wave: if you felt all that pain and inconvenience and frustration—a bonked head, scraped belly, stolen breath, like a blow to the stomach, and lungful of salt water—if you felt that from anything else, from a mugger, for instance, there would be no joy in it at all, only fear, resentment, and hate. But because the wipe-out is part of the great play of waves, you laugh. Now I'm not saying we should laugh if we're mugged, but there are other waves in life that we can laugh at even when we wipe-out. But we don't laugh because we forget that we're body-surfing in God.

Laughing at yourself ("what an idiot!") is one of the very healthiest things you can ever do, physically, emotionally, and spiritually.

When you're married, your greatest playing field should be your bed. Sex is one of God's biggest waves. How awful not to play in it, not to laugh at it even when you wipe-out! There are books that make sex so solemn and serious that they turn play into work. Much work should be turned into play, but no play should be turned into work. Those books do as much harm as pornography. They *are* a kind of pornography. I'll bet their authors had performance anxiety in their sandboxes.

120. What It Means to Be Pro-Life

It means what Moses said, to "just say yes" to life, to "choose life."

"Life" means much more than just biological survival. It means all the levels of human life, from the biological to the psychological to the interpersonal to the religious.

Therefore to be "pro-life" means:

1. loving and caring for your bodily health and the health of the planet that nourishes it
2. loving and caring for play, that up-rush of life that we share with the higher animals but not with the lower (that's why we play with dogs, not with worms)
3. loving and caring for other human biological lives, not killing them by abortion, euthanasia, suicide, or starting wars
4. loving and caring for other human psychological and spiritual lives as you care for your own, loving others as you love yourself

5. loving the moral law that tells you how to do that
6. knowing and loving nature and the nature of everything: man, woman, animals, God, and even sister death; not acting against their natures but "painting with the grain"
7. loving the source and inventor of all life wherever He comes to you: in nature, in conscience, in the Bible, in the Mass, in children, everywhere, even in death

You see? Being pro-life is bigger than #3 alone.

121. The Inner Zoo

You can take a trip to the zoo any day, in any weather. Just look inside yourself.

You will find both good and bad animals of all kinds running around in your inner cages. Play with the good ones, and keep the bad ones caged.

Nobody is so good that they don't have any snakes. But they often cover them up. That's understandable.

Nobody is so bad that they don't have any bunnies. But they often cover them up. That's incomprehensible.

122. Dying is Easy

Dying is much easier than living. You don't have to do anything! It's like a sacrament: it's given to you. By death, God made it easy to do what we find very hard to do while we're living: total surrender, giving back the gift of life we received, the foundational gift for all others.

At the end of your life, you become a priest, just once. You say Mass, and you offer God the Host of your body, saying: "This is my body." If you are a baptized Christian, and thus part of the body of Christ, Christ says that Mass, and it is part of Christ's body that you offer when you die in Christ. (But Christ's body is not cut up into parts; each part contains the whole Christ. That's true of each wafer of the Eucharist and each member of the Church.)

And your blood—that is His blood, because He got it from Mary, and she got it from Eve and so did you, so His blood is your blood and your blood is His blood. There is only one human blood supply. Because of Eve and Mary, His blood is your blood.

"In the blood is the life." So when you die, you also offer your blood, your life, now separated from your body, just as Christ does in the Eucharist, which separates His blood and His body. You do it not only "just *as*" Christ does it, you do it as *part* of what Christ does, what Christ is doing now. (Don't ask "What would Jesus do?" Ask "What is Jesus doing?")

123. "Blessed Are the Poor"

We believe many things that contradict our feelings: that some foods that taste great are not good for us (like candy) and that some that taste terrible are (like spinach). We trust the experts, the scientists, doctors, and dieticians. How foolish not to trust God when He tells us things that contradict our feelings, like "blessed are the poor."

It's easier to believe God when He tells us things that contradict our *senses* (e.g., that that little thing that looks like a wafer of bread is really Jesus) or that seem to contradict our *reason* (e.g., that Jesus is simultaneously God and man) than it is to believe Him when He tells us things that contradict our *feelings*, especially our desires (e.g., that poverty is blessed and that riches are dangerous).

But what He says is either true or false, and if it's false, then it's dishonest to pretend it's true. Let's just blow up the cathedrals as the biggest lie in history. But if it is true, then we'd better know it and live it, like a doctor's prescription.

If the poor are blessed, then let's stop envying the rich, and let's stop complaining when we've been blessed with a little poverty. If we had been rich, we would have missed that blessing! Let's thank God for all our blessings, including that one, even though it doesn't feel like a blessing.

Why doesn't it feel like a blessing? Because we are fools. That's another one of the surprising things He has told us.

124. Surfing Wisdom

Life is made of waves. (Everything is.) It comes in crests and troughs. It's easy to ride the crests; the real test is the troughs. Expect them. Ride them out. That's part of our job description. Imagine a fire fighter who was surprised, angry, and resentful every time the fire alarm bell rang.

125. The Beauty of Sadness

"Nobody gets out of here alive," says Jim Morrison.

"They give birth astride a grave," says Samuel Beckett. In other words, as soon as we're born, we begin to die.

Our greatest dramas are tragedies. Our greatest music is in a minor key. Our most beautiful colors are dark colors. The best definition of our greatest art is "that which has the power to break your heart."

Some curse God for putting such sadness into beauty. I thank Him for putting such beauty into sadness.

126. Have Kids

Having fits is much more rational than having kids. Have kids anyway.

Kids will break your heart. That's part of the plan. Only a broken heart beats in tune with God's heart. (Look at a crucifix until you understand that.)

Kids will also break the bank, break your budget. That's part of the plan, too.

Almost everyone should have kids. Why? Because only when you live for someone else, do you really live. Only when you work for the happiness of someone you love, can you be really happy. And if you can't love your own kids, you can't love anybody.

If you don't have kids but you do have a spouse, there's only one person in the world more important than yourself: your spouse. That's less complete than having kids, because even in God the Holy Trinity, there's two others, not just one, for each person to love.

127. "What Can We Do to Make You Happy?"

I'm going to sound dramatic here, not just to get your attention but to be realistic. I'm going to ask you to perform the thought experiment of imagining you are at my bedside as I am dying. Someday you will have to perform this, not in thought but in life.

You ask me: "What can I do for you? What would make you happiest?"

I answer: Three things. First, love your mother. Second, love your spouse. Third, love your kids.

Be patient with all three of them. They all have to be patient with you in ways you do not understand. If you don't understand *that*, then think: do *they* understand all the ways *you* have to be patient with them? No. Well, then, isn't it very likely that this works both ways?

It's hard to be patient. "Only love makes it possible, and only perfect love makes it a joy." (That's from the old Catholic marriage ceremony.) To love people, you need even more than patience, you need to understand them, you need to get inside their souls, inside their lives. And that makes patience easier.

This is one of the things we'll be doing in Heaven forever—understanding each other—so we'd better get in as much practice as possible here. Life is spring training.

128. The Most Precious Gift

The most precious gift you give to someone you love is time. Where you choose to spend it when you are free is the surest indicator of what and whom you love.

Time is a precious commodity because no one can give you anymore of it; no one can give you a 25th hour in any day or replenish the past time you have spent.

Except God. For He lives in eternity, and He can multiply our little loaves and fishes of time. But only the ones we give away to Him.

129. Sacrifices

Here are five reasons for making sacrifices

1. You cannot live a complete human life without them. Be prepared to make them. Do not be surprised or resentful at them.
2. They are your opportunity to get closer to Christ than anything else on earth can give you.
3. In Heaven, the ones who will shine the brightest will not be the people who shone in the spotlight on earth but the obscure, unnoticed, and forgotten "little givers." Unlike most of the rich and famous, they didn't put themselves first. (That's why they weren't rich and famous.) We have been promised by the very highest Authority that the first will be last and the last will be first.
4. Even on earth, the givers shine the brightest, inside. Look at their eyes.

5. The alternative to sacrifice is Hell: selfishness and ego-tism.

This is logical: Heaven is being with God and God is love, and love sacrifices, so it's a package deal: Heaven, God, love, and sacrifice. The alternative to Heaven is Hell; therefore, the alternative to sacrifice is Hell.

You can be a nonsacrificer and still be quite nice, polite, and acceptable in this fallen world. You needn't kill anybody. You needn't even bother anybody. You just demand that nobody else bother you.

130. Trickling to the Sea

Every act we perform is like a drop of water. When water drops join, they become trickles, then streams, then rivers. All rivers seek the sea.

We act in certain directions, as water flows in certain directions. When you cast your eyes around the room looking for your shoelaces, you seek them because you want to tie your shoe, to walk to the car, to go to the post office, to buy stamps, to mail a check to the credit card company, to pay for a new tent, to go camping, to enjoy nature. Finally, you come to an end, to something that's not trickling to some further end.

Our lives are filled with many little rivers. Their number keeps increasing. More and more efficient means—but to what end? We don't even ask! We should spend more time at the sea, both literally and allegorically: we should spend more time enjoying ends rather than means. For only the end justifies the means; that's what "means" *means*: a means to an end. Good ends don't justify evil means, but good ends do justify good means.

When we work, we are in rivers. When we play, we are in some bay or inlet of the sea. Working is fresh water, playing is salt water: a foretaste of Heaven.

But what is the sea? What is our final end? What is Heaven? What is the meaning of life? What's it all about, Alfie?

It must exist because if it didn't, we wouldn't seek it. We are all water seeking the sea. We are restless until we rest in it.

And it must be complete, one great total thing, something bigger than we've ever had. For otherwise, the little bays and inlets of it that we do already experience would be enough for us, and they would never bore us no matter how long we stayed in them. But they, too, move us onward, beyond ourselves. They confess that they are only little bays of the great sea.

This is my favorite proof for the existence of God.

131. An Unnecessary Book

How unnecessary a book like this is! You already know everything in it. If not, how come you recognize that it's true as soon as you read it?

But it's also necessary because we forget what we know and need reminders. We're all absentminded.

132. Uniqueness

Be good, but be you.

Be you, but be good.

The basic patterns of goodness are the same for everyone. They are obligatory; God did not give Moses the ten suggestions.

The patterns for you-ness are yours alone. God didn't make any clones, only kids.

133. God Has Children But No Grandchildren

Not only didn't God make any clones, He didn't even make any grandchildren; He let us do that. We can make you born, but only God can make you born again. You can't get God from your parents; you have to get Him yourself, firsthand. He gives you Himself with His own hands, in the Eucharist

And you have to get yourself there, too.

134. The Meaning of Sunlight

What is sunlight? It speaks; it says something; it is a word from the sun of God.

If it's a word, why isn't the word clearer? Why isn't the word spoken by the sun as clear to our minds as its light is to our eyes? Because it would kill us if it was.

Pet a bird and you will understand. You have to temper your affection or else you will kill it. You can't hug a bird as you can hug a dog. Sunlight is God's tempered love, one of His gentle pettings to us, His delicate little birds.

Only the angels can endure His big hugs. They are like His dogs.

And only He Himself can endure His full love: that's why He has to be three persons, not just one.

135. Work and Play— and Roses

Do more of both. But don't play so much that you don't work or work so much that you don't play.

Some people are lazy and hate to work and only want to play. That's not surprising. Play is fun. What's surprising is that some people hate to play. Why?

Some work so hard that they have no *time to feel* anymore. Some feelings (like anger) don't require much time to cultivate; others (like compassion) do. Maybe that's why these people work so much: to distract themselves from their emotional emptiness. They're afraid that they're becoming like robots. So what do they do about it? They act more like robots.

What else could they do? They could just forget time for a while and take a walk. That way, they would confront "itselfness." The rose you stop to smell is not a thing you classify, compare, calculate, buy, and use. It is just itself.

This is not irresponsible and childish. Just the opposite. For other people are like roses. They each have itselfness, and you have to take time just to sit and listen to them. They all have thorns, and they're all beautiful. Really seeing roses is good training for really seeing people.

136. Natural Time

Everything in nature and everything in life has its natural time and tempo. Find it and ride with it, like riding a wave. Catch it at the breaking point or you won't catch it at all. You can't hurry anything alive, anything growing. Sometimes you can stop it, or delay it, though. You can even kill it. And you should, when the growing thing is something bad like cancer or sin. But with everything else, find its rhythm and ride it like a horse or a wave.

137. Why the Good Suffer

Because the world is so beautiful.

God is love, and that's why He made the world so un-
bearably beautiful. And because this world is so beautiful
and we are so foolish, there is the danger that any of the
things in this beautiful world may become so much a part of
our identity, so satisfying, so homelike to our souls that
when we die, we become ghosts, unable to leave our old
houses. So He has to detach us from them by pain, as well
as attaching us to them by pleasure. We need both. So He
gives us both.

He could have made the world less beautiful in the first
place, and then we would have needed less pain for our de-
tachment from it. (You don't feel pain when you move out
of an ugly motel room, but you feel pain when you move
out of your beautiful old house.) But God's heart, like our
deepest heart, preferred the package deal of the agony *and*

the ecstasy, the bitter *and* the sweet, the heights *and* the depths, rather than the flat, dull, safe middle road.

Our mother's womb must grow confining as our life within it grows larger, both in body and in mind. The world is our second womb. If it did not grow confining and small, we would not want to be born again.

138. What We Want Most of All

What we all want most of all is to hear these words: "You are simply the most precious thing in the world to me. In all possible worlds, I would love you. I would wait a thousand lifetimes for you. I would give up the whole world for you. You are the center of my life, my heart, and my mind, and there could never be any possible rival."

This is every lover's dream, and we are all lovers. We are designed by love for love. And our dream will come true in Heaven because we will hear these words from our Beloved, the One who never lies.

Since we already know this, we are already responsible for doing it. We've been told our lines, and we have to rehearse.

Saying "we *have to* rehearse" makes it sound like a law. And it is! We are so stupid that God had to make this joy, this dream, this ecstasy a *law:* "Thou *shalt* love, thou *shalt* experience the dream of thy heart; I command you to dance the dance of ecstasy." It's like ordering a man to make love to a beautiful woman.

I think in Heaven we will have an incredible laughing fit when we look back and see this: that we were so stupid that God had to give us a moral *law* to get us to make love.

139. Four Things to Make You Happy

I've always found these four to work. They are not *ideas* but real *things*.

First, there is a mysterious but powerful source of happiness and even energy in four things in nature that are free and easily available, four things that contain a lot of happiness juice:

- the sky, the sun (but dark and stormy skies, too), the moon, the stars, and clouds (all kinds of clouds), and weather (all kinds of weather)—everything that comes down from the sky (there's wisdom in the ancient confusion between Heaven and "the heavens")
- the sea, waves, and rivers, and all kinds of water, even lakes, ponds, and backyard swimming pools (water is God's second favorite thing, after light; the second thing He created)
- trees, forests, swaths of greenery (rolling hills, too, waves made of land), and, of course, mountains

- animals—just petting a cat or letting a dog love you works little puffs of magic

Second, people are even bigger happiness-factories than animals. Do a good deed to someone, something surprising. Go out of your way to help someone. Figure out some little new, creative way to spell love. Everyone knows this works like crazy. You have to be crazy to forget it. Most of us are.

Third, in order to feel good about yourself, be totally honest with yourself. Say "no" to all the big and little lies, hidings and excuses, compromises, and shuffling little dances we are all so clever in doing. Crack the brittle shell we all secrete around ourselves. Strip your soul naked for the embrace of God's truth. This can be as exhilarating and is always as liberating, as stripping naked for sex.

Fourth, open up to the first cause of all happiness: practice the presence of God.

These four deeds don't take any energy. They give you energy. Then don't even take much time. They give you time.

140. Pages Stuck Together

These two pages of my little notebook stuck together, so I can't write on them. Everything happens for a reason. Sometimes the reason is to remind us that we don't know the reason.

141. How Communion Works

In it God says to you: Put the lips of your faith to my heart and drink my blood. It alone will save your life. I give my life for yours in this holy exchange, this holy communion. I suck the sin, the poison, out of your heart, if you let me. Open your heart to my lips and I will do it. And open your lips to my heart and I will give you a blood transfusion.

142. Don't Balance

Life is not a seesaw. Don't try to balance career and family, or money and family, or self and family. Don't even think that way. To balance means to compromise. Never compromise your family. They are the *reason* for your career, your money, and even yourself: you have been created *for them* and trained to be you *for them*. What good are all the jobs, armies, and politics in the world except to preserve and protect the life of families? That's "where it's at," that's the center of life. Everything else is on the periphery. That's the fulcrum, everything else is the seesaw. Try to balance everything else; don't try to balance the fulcrum.

143. "Pay It Forward"

The word "piety" originally meant two things: loyalty to family and to God, or the gods. The connection is this: you can't pay back what you have been given by either one: life itself. So you have to "pay it forward." Pass on the gift. You can't repay your Creator or your procreators, so you pay your children instead, as your parents did. What a great system God invented! How much better than "justice" or "equality" or "rights"!

144. When Everything Seems Senseless

Look what happened to Abraham. God apparently took away the most precious thing in his life, Isaac. God apparently took back His own best gift and gave no explanation or compensation.

Terrible things happen and not just to heroes like Abraham. And when they do, we have to make the choice Abraham had to make: Do I go on trusting this mysterious God even though I can't understand Him, can't understand His reasons, can't understand why He let this terrible thing happen to me, this thing that seems to make no sense at all? He certainly had the power to arrange for it not to happen, yet He didn't. Do I trust Him despite that or not?

This "that" may be anything, small or large, from accident to personal failure, from depression to death, or worse. There are many things in life worse than death. Despair, divorce, betrayal, and insanity can all be worse than death. Even death can be worse than death if it happens not to you but to someone you love more than you love yourself.

Why does He take *this* away?

It's clearly a test. But it's utterly *un*clear why He gives the test to one and not to another. But it's very clear what the right answer to the test is. The right answer is "yes."

Yes, I trust you even if you take *this* away, take this Isaac. For you are not a means to *this*, or to anything else. My trust in you is not conditional upon your providing *this* to me. You are not a divine machine designed to supply *this*. I will trust you even though I cannot understand. I have no proof that you are good, but I have the power to choose to believe that you are good. And by this power I choose you. My choice is unconditional and nonnegotiable and irrevocable.

If someone asks you "Why?"—if you ask yourself "Why? Why such total trust?"—the answer is Jesus. The trust is not irrational, even though we can't give a reason for it. For we *got* a reason for it. *God* gave us the reason for it. Jesus is our reason. Or He is our substitute for having our own reason, for figuring it out, as the ram was the substitute for Isaac in Genesis 22. If God had not sent Jesus but remained invisible and far away—if God had not showed us His love with such shattering concreteness that our innocence shattered like glass before His bleeding feet—it would still be possible for heroes of faith like Abraham to trust Him, but much harder for weaklings like us. So He gave us Jesus as our reason. Jesus is our crutch; Jesus is our religion. Of course religion is a crutch, for we are cripples.

So when everything seems senseless and your faith is tested and God puts you on Job's dung heap, there is nothing better than to look at a crucifix (which is much worse than a dung heap!) and say "Jesus, I trust you." Maybe it won't make sense to anyone else. And it won't make the pain go away. He doesn't *want* the pain to go away—not yet; He *sent* it. But He wants to hear those words from you. He *longs* to hear those words, He has a lover's passion to hear those words. The harder they are to say, the more precious they are.

145. The Wisdom of Childhood

I used to be wise. Then I grew up.

When I was about eight, I think, I formulated my first general philosophical principle: "a little understanding is better than a lot of long-suffering." I still think that's one of the best rules for a happy marriage. It's probably even a good rule for international diplomacy.

At about the same age, driving home from church one Sunday morning and having been confused about something I was taught in Sunday School, I checked it out with my father, who I knew was wise in the ways of God.

"Dad, all that stuff we learn we're supposed to do in church and Sunday School—it's all just one thing, isn't it?"

He was rightly suspicious of childish oversimplifications, so he said, "What do you mean? What one thing?"

"Well, we just have to ask Jesus what He wants us to do and then do it, right?"

I can still remember his look of pleased surprise. "Yes, that's right, son. You're right." My father was a wise man. *He* was probably wiser at the age of eight, too.

At about the same age, I lusted after an expensive Lionel electric train for Christmas. I had never received such an expensive present, and I was afraid my father couldn't afford it. I probably pestered him for many days before he sat me down, a few days before Christmas and said,

"Son, do you know what Christmas means?"

"I think so."

"Tell me, then."

"It's about love."

"Right. And why do we have it on December 25th?"

"I don't know."

"I think you do. Whose birthday is that?"

"Jesus."

"Right. So what does Jesus' birth have to do with love?"

"I don't know."

"I'll give you a hint. Why do we give gifts to each other on Christmas?"

"Because we love each other."

"Good! Now what does that have to do with Jesus' birth?"

"God gave us Jesus on Christmas because He loves us."

"Good! You know the meaning of Christmas. So you know why your mother and I give you gifts, right?"

"Because you love me."

"Right. Now suppose we can't afford to give you that expensive Lionel train you want so much. Would you still know we love you?"

At this point my selfish little calculating brain went into panic mode. Which answer would get me the train? Could I blackmail him into buying it for me if I said no? That didn't feel right somehow. I just couldn't figure out what answer would work, so I did what most kids do in a last resort emergency: when all else fails, tell the truth. "Sure, Dad, I know you love me even if you can't afford to buy me the train."

"Thank you, Son. You've made me very happy."

But *I* wasn't happy, because I thought I had given up the train and given him a way out of having to buy it for me. But on Christmas morning there it was, under the tree.

Well, the train is rusting away in the attic and not running anymore. But Dad's lesson and his love are still running round my track with a full head of steam.

146. Better Than Right

It's better to be happy than to be right.

Here's my proof. Making others happy makes it easier for them to be good, and being happy yourself makes it easier for you to be good. But being in the right but unhappy makes other people unhappy and that makes it harder for them to be good.

If you think that demeans righteousness, remember that the only way you can be really happy is by being righteous, being good.

147. My Obsession

Everyone has at least one weakness, one blind spot, one obsession. Mine is computers. Everything digital is my enemy.

I am a calm and reasonable person most of the time. But every time I try to tame that beast that thinks so differently than me, I and *it* turn out to be in the same relationship as matter and antimatter or Count Dracula and Doctor Van Helsing. And *it* always wins. *It* is the Yankees and I am the Red Sox. *It* always finds new ways to beat me. *It* is Lucy and I am Charlie Brown. *It* always changes the rules, snatching away the football just as I'm about to kick it. *It* is the tree and I am the kite.

Not only does *it* beat me physically, but also spiritually: *it* turns me into a mad demon lusting after its blood and screaming, "The hell of Gates shall not prevail against Peter!"

So I confess to the world (or that tiny segment of it that reads this) that I am quite insane in this one area of life. I am a devil full of fire and blood-lust, longing to inflict torture, dismemberment, death, and destruction on the hell of Gates. If a giant nuclear bomb exploded just above my head right now, I would die in a calmer state of mind than the state of the five D's: dastardly digital-delivered doom and despair. In fact, I think I would look up at the bomb and say, "Well, that's the way it is. Shit happens. That's our fate. I can take it. I'm a Red Sox fan." But that damned little machine is supposed to serve us and obey us, unlike bombs, which are *supposed* to kill us. It's our robot, and *it* has become my Frankenstein's monster.

If I went to Hell, all the computers there would laugh at me. That's where they're programmed. That's where they all go when they "go down." Down to the war room in Hell to plan new unpredictables, like those monsters that jump out at you in video games. Down to plot against our sanity, our souls, and our peace. Down to show us who's boss.

I curse them with the maximal Mongolian curse: may a diseased yak with dripping hemorrhoids mistake your mother's face for a toilet bowl! But computers wouldn't care. Alas, they have no mothers. No mother could have designed motherboards. Mothers have compassion.

I think I'll stop now before I complete the case for my incarceration.

148. Reasons

Most of us do most of the things we do, even the good things we do, for reasons that aren't that good. We should keep doing good things, but we should have better reasons for doing them.

Here are two lists of reasons: good reasons for doing things and bad reasons for doing things.

Seven Bad Reasons for Doing Anything

1. It's popular. (So?)
2. It's modern. (So what?)
3. It's efficient. (For what?)
4. It's economical. (Is it, really?)
5. It's just "what's done." (So what's your point?)
6. It's necessary. (No, it isn't, unless it's God. There's only one necessary being.)
7. I have to do this. (Are you a robot or a slave?)

Seven Good Reasons for Doing Anything

1. God loves it.
2. I love it.
3. It's good.
4. It's true.
5. It's beautiful.
6. It makes me happy.
7. It makes someone else happy.

See how simple it is to change your life?

149. If God Became a Cat

If God became a cat instead of a man, wouldn't you revere cats?

Well, God became a man. Why don't we revere man more?

If He had said, "Whatever you do to one of the least of these my cats, you do to me," would we go around dissing and dismissing cats? No, we'd see God every time we looked at the littlest kitty cat.

Too bad we don't revere each other as well as we'd revere cats.

150. The Big Picture

Always look for the big picture.

Lack of the big picture is why it's hard for many Catholics to understand why the Church forbids so many things that so many reasonable people in the world don't, like divorce, fornication, contraception, masturbation, sodomy, euthanasia, and cloning. The principle behind all these no's is the same yes, the same "big picture": "What God has joined together in designing creation, let no man put asunder." When God uses glue, don't use scissors. God glued together personal union and procreation, and man cuts them apart with the scissors of contraception and cloning, which are two sides of the same coin. God glued together sex and marriage, and man cuts them apart in fornication and masturbation. God glued together body and soul in creating us, and man cuts them apart in all killing, including euthanasia. God glued babies and mothers together, and man cuts them apart in abortion. God glued husband and wife together, and man cuts them apart in divorce. God glued male and female together, and man cuts them apart in homosexuality. The "big picture" lets you see the connections. And it lets you see that it's only because the right thing is so very good that the wrong thing is bad.

All but one of these controversial moral issues is about sex. That's not because the Church is obsessed with sex, it's because the culture is. The Church has never changed her orthodoxy, the world just changes its heresies. In the fourth century no one questioned her sexual morality, but even the fishmongers and wine makers were arguing about the two natures of Christ and the persons in the Trinity. In the 16th and 17th centuries, the controversies weren't about sex, but about faith and works, church and state, the Bible and sacraments. In the 18th century, the most controversial moral issue was *duelling*!

History gives you a sense of perspective.

151. What Acts Change the World the Most?

So you want to change the world and you wonder where to start? Pray.

"More things are wrought by prayer than this world dreams of." If God showed us all the differences all our prayers made to all the lives they affected, down through the generations, we'd never be able to get up off our knees again for the rest of our lives.

God hides many good things from us for our own good.

Prayer is an act. When you pray, you *do* something, you change something, you make something new, like building, repairing, or demolishing a house. It's not just a good exercise for *you*, it builds, repairs, or demolishes a real thing out there. And a lot of things out there need to be built, repaired, or demolished.

The difference between prayer and construction work is that we can't see the buildings our prayers construct because we can't see the Master Builder anymore than the tools can see the carpenter. We are His tools.

If He wanted to, He could make Himself and all His works visible. But then we wouldn't need faith anymore, and that would weaken our prayers, our acts of building.

152. Seven Questions, One Answer

1. How to live?
2. How to be wise?
3. How to be good?
4. How to overcome fear?
5. How to pray?
6. How to be grateful and, therefore, happy?
7. How to be ready to die?

Seven rather important questions. Apparently, simple answers are inadequate.

Wrong. *Un*simple answers are inadequate. The maximal answers to the maximal questions are always maximally simple. The answer to all seven questions (and many more) is the same single word. That's the word He spoke to Moses from the burning bush: "I AM." That word, in Hebrew, is so holy that no Jew will ever speak it. It's God's prerogative to utter His own name. We only "practice the presence" of this God. His is the mouth; ours are the ears.

But instead of just saying it, let me try to explain the "big picture" so that you can see it, not just say it.

Start with the fact that only atheists deny: God is real and present and knows everything and, therefore, is looking at you right now, knowing absolutely everything about you. You have His full attention! He designed your soul, so He knows everything in it: He knew it into existence.

He doesn't let you see Him because if you did, if you saw Him as He really is, you would not be able to eat, sleep, or speak coherently. You would be immersed in such a sea of intoxicating glory that you would just go gaga or maybe melt away. When Peter, James, and John saw Jesus' divine glory on the Mount of Transfiguration, Peter "did not know what he was saying" and blabbered some idiotic plans for making the place a tourist trap. The other two were unable to say anything at all. Ask any of the canonized saints to define or even describe the God they saw in their mystical visions. Ask any one of the 20 million Americans who have had an out-of-body experience or a near-death-experience and actually *met* the "being of light," and *knew* that He knew them totally and absolutely and yet loved them totally and absolutely. They all say this experience can't be put into words. Experiencing this presence always causes total joy, total certainty, and total fearlessness, even of death (*especially* of death). And it changes their whole life, for they all now see the same truth very clearly: they see that only two things in this world matter, only two things have absolute value, for only two things last forever, and, therefore, only these two things are worth caring about: truth and love. That's what God is made of: God (the Father) *is* truth (the Son, the word, the logos, the reason or mind of God) and

God *is* love (the Spirit that unites the Father and the Son). That's the doctrine of the Trinity in one sentence.

There is a great power in simply remembering and believing that He is real and really present, really looking at you. (That's essentially all that "practicing the presence of God" means.) But we have to be very "interferingly" concrete and dangerously intimate, not politely abstract and safely faraway. God is not "aware of us," watching us "from a distance." He is looking at you right now, right there in front of you, a foot from your face, like a mother gazing intently into her baby's face.

It takes too long to say it, so it starts to look complicated; but it's the simplest thing in the world. Brother Lawrence, who called it "the practice of the presence of God" in that beloved little book by that name, was so unintelligent that he couldn't be trusted with the simplest tasks, like buying food or holding horses. He had very bad attention deficit disorder (ADD). And God used this simple-minded man to write a simple-minded book, a beginner-type book about how to pray and how to live. My little book *Prayer for Beginners* is almost a plagiarism of that one.

Muslims speak of "gaflah" (forgetfulness). It's their version of original sin: an innate, universal human tendency to forget God. That's why they all pray five times a day: because they know they have spiritual ADD. Good for them. We can do the same without becoming Muslims. Just turn and meet His gaze.

But be warned. It might hurt. Especially when you see the prints of the nails in His hands, the tears in His eyes, and the brokenness of His heart that were caused by your sins. But it is good hurt. It is the beginning of your purgatory.

The holy Cure of Ars noticed a peasant spending hours in church before the blessed sacrament in adoration. He asked the peasant what he did when he prayed, and the answer was the best definition I know of contemplation: "I just look at Him and He just looks at me."

He's really there, you know, and He really waits for us, for our attention. (Attention is an act of love.) And if we just turn and say "hello," "thanks," and "I love you" many times, then He will act many times, He will change us, He will *do things to us*, like a great invisible tide turning and raising a fleet of stranded ships stuck on sandbars, moving the million-ton vessels gradually and imperceptibly but effortlessly and irresistibly. (All the greatest powers in the universe are invisible.)

So do that: practice His presence and then those seven most important questions of life will be answered. I guarantee it. Try it, you'll like it.

But you really have to do it, not just think about doing it, or agree that you ought to do it. It's amazing how easily we can convince ourselves that we're doing it when we're only resolving to do it. Perhaps that's the terrible temptation of the intellectual. Alas, both you and I are intellectuals.

153. The Practical Solution to the Problem of Evil

There are two kinds of evil: sin and suffering, the evil that comes to us and the evil that comes from us.

The first kind harms only the body; the second kind is worse because it harms the soul.

The practical solution to the first kind is easy: say yes (in trust: transform it by trust into something good). The practical solution to the second kind is hard: say no.

God gave us the essential solution to sin, and we are to do what He did. First, He sent us the Savior, then He sent us the Sanctifier. First the Son, then the Spirit. He loves sinners (that's why He sent the Savior), but He hates sins (that's why He sent the Sanctifier). We're to do the same.

How?

There are three possible answers, three possible attitudes we can have to our own sins.

1. We can hate the sin only a little bit. That's easy, and cheap, and does nothing.

2. We can hate the sinner as well as the sin. That's easy, too, and does something, all right: it does harm. We're commanded to "love your neighbor as yourself," so that means we also have to love ourselves as we love our neighbors. And we're not supposed to hate them, so we're not supposed to hate ourselves either.
3. The hardest answer is the only one that works: love the sinner (the self) more *and* hate the sin more. Be like God: passionately in love with the sinner and passionately in hate with the sin.

That's easy to say and think but hard to do. We have to love the sinner much, much more and the sin much, much less at the same time and for the same reason, as God does. Instead, we tend to love the sinner just a little more and the sin just a little less. But that doesn't do much. Because when we love the sinner (the self) only a little more, we tend to love the sin, too, and when we hate the sin only a little more, we tend to hate the sinner (the self), too. Thus a weak version of answer #3 comes back to answer #1 or answer #2. The only version of #3 that works is the strong version.

We should be *passionately* impatient with our sins. They should be more than a matter of life and death to us, because they *are*. They kill our souls, just as diseases kill our bodies. We use masks, antibiotics, and even condoms to avoid contracting deadly diseases; we should do no less for our souls.

And we should be *passionately* in love with our true selves, our heavenly destiny. If we saw the bright, glorious things we are destined to be, we would find it intolerable to be anything less.

The first line of defense against sin is thought. "Fuggetaboutit!" Don't even *think* about it. "Sow a thought, reap an act; sow an act, reap a habit; sow a habit, reap a character; sow a character, reap a destiny." Winning the war at this first line of defense is much easier and less costly than repairing the damage later. See sin for what it is: shit. Flush it as soon as you smell it.

154. Handicaps

Every person in the world is handicapped. The only difference is not between the handicapped and the non-handicapped, but only between one kind of handicap and another.

Everyone has at least one unique plus and at least one unique minus. Both are there for sharing. Handicaps do not always work for the perfecting of individuals but they always work for the perfecting of relationships. Perfect, complete, nonhandicapped individuals could never form deep relationships because they'd have no deep needs.

For one thing, they would be hermaphroditic, because men need women (I know) and women need men (I guess). Men are handicapped for not being women and women are handicapped for not being men.

And if men are womanly men, they're handicapped for not being manly men, and if women are manly women, they're handicapped for not being womanly women.

Men are laughably incompetent at femininity, and women are laughably incompetent at masculinity. They're both incompetent at even understanding it, much less being it!

Men are totally superior to women—at being men. And women are totally superior to men—at being women.

I know some of my handicaps. I have ADD. I am an intellectually bright but emotionally dense, absent-minded professor whose most remarkable talent is messing up somehow at everything except the few things I do well, but only one at a time. Mom is a classy, sassy, sexy, dazzlingly intelligent, self-giving, omnicompetent, multitasking, octopussing, practical problem-solver. I never quite grew up; she never really had a childhood. I'll be 12 when I die, she was 40 when she was born. We are Mars and Venus, Mutt and Jeff, Laurel and Hardy, the Odd Couple, a comedy of errors. All couples are Odd Couples. God gave us each other to laugh at and to learn to love-despite-everything as well as to love-because-of-everything.

The result of this chaos? "Here, let me do this for you." You hear those words a lot in schools for the handicapped, but not very often in other schools, especially the "best" schools. The "best" of us are the worst at knowing they're handicapped. That makes them the most handicapped of all.

155. Why Bad Days Are Good

There will be days when you will feel you are on top of the world, and there are days you will feel the world is on top of you. How you act when you feel like an ape is much more important than how you act when you feel like an angel—more important for shaping the person you are making yourself into, the person you will be on that third kind of day, the commonest kind of day, when you feel neither high nor low, neither angel nor ape.

The good choices you make when your feelings don't back you up, the good choices you make on bad days, are made by that part of you that will still be there tomorrow, the part that sits in the captain's chair. The good choices you make on good days, when it's easy to make them, are made mainly by good feelings, which are only guests in the captain's cabin. They won't be there tomorrow.

Feeling-borne choices are like wind-borne gliders. They are exhilarating to ride, but the wind will die down tomorrow, and if you don't have in interior engine working, the plane won't get off the ground tomorrow.

Feelings are to the will what crutches are to the legs. Don't rely on spiritual prosthetics.

156. Our Dyslexia

We say our God is #1, spouse is #2, kids are #3, friends are #4, job is #5, and dog is #6, but we give more time and affection to the dog than to God. Maybe we treat dog like God because we're dyslexic.

157. We Are Designed to Burn

When you make a fire in the woods, you direct everything to that little flame to make it grow and not fade. That's the whole point of the fuel, the fireplace, the matches, the draft, the protection against the wind, and the protection against the rain.

That's what our lives look like from Heaven's point of view. God sends His angels to guard us like hands cupped around the tiny, feeble, frail, and fragile flame of little love that He has ignited in our lives, to shelter that flame from the winds and rains of the evil spirits who want to put it out. Around each of the many little loves, prayers, and sacrifices in our lives, there are unimaginably fierce winds blowing from both Heaven and Hell: the first, to fan the flame, and the second, to extinguish it. Meanwhile, we sit cupped in the hands of providence and angels, and Heaven holds its breath to see whether we will let the flame go out or give it fuel.

The fuel is our very selves. We are designed to burn, with a flame that is eternal.

158. Simple-Hearted

When John, the youngest of the 12 apostles, was getting old (he lived into his nineties), his disciples complained that he only talked about one thing: love. His reply: "There isn't anything else." You get simple when you get old.

That's because there's no time for anything else. Time is running out. You either get simple-minded or simple-hearted. Simple-minded is mentally defective; simple-hearted is wise.

Simple is wise because the meaning of life is simpler than we are. We mess up because we forget the simple truths, not because we forget the complex ones. Nobody ever ruined lives because they forgot Einstein; they ruined lives because they forgot Moses.

All of us, deep down, know that the meaning of life is just one word, and all of us, deep down, know what word that is.

So we're wiser than we think, but we don't want to admit it because that makes us responsible for doing it. Complex-ifying is a great cop-out. Excuses are always complex.

What we know is that the soul of everything is one thing and that that is love, even though the bodies and the appearances of those things are many things and they don't all look like love.

The heart of everything is love because everything is created by love. There is only one first cause, and He *is* love. Therefore, everything He does, He does for love. Everything He makes, He makes out of love. Everything He allows, He allows because of love.

We have to learn how to be like that.

159. Why So Much Religion?

I'm coming to the end of this little book of essential advice for living the rest of your life. Why has so much of it been about religion? Why not politics, humanistic psychology, economics, or science?

Because "religion" means "relationship" (literally), and life is, at its heart, relationships. Buber says "all real living is meeting." Relationships make things important; things don't make relationships important.

And because if it's not true that all human relationships find their source and summit in God, who designed them, if God isn't the key to understanding them and perfecting them, why then is God not God, God is only a Zeus or a Santa Claus, a myth.

And because God *is* a relationship, a family, a Trinity.

There's so much *about* religion because there's so much *in* religion. Unless it's not true, in which case it's the world's biggest lie and you'd better become an honest atheist. The one thing it can't possibly be is moderately important. Its claims are too big for that: if it isn't more than everything, it's less than nothing.

I didn't choose to make this book so "religious" because I'm "into religion" or because I'm so "religious." I'm not. I find it harder to keep my mind on God than on thousands of other things. I have to force myself to pray even for a few minutes. I don't have to force myself to watch a ball game for a few minutes or even for a few hours.

Do as I say, not as I do. (Every honest parent says that.)

160. Why Do Bad Things Happen to Good People?

When bad times come, when bad things happen, we probe for causes: Why did this happen? Did God do it? What did I do wrong? Who's to blame? What can I do to fix it?

But all that usually does no good, because the past is dead and can't be changed. Only the future can, by present choices. So ask instead: What use can I now make of this bad thing? *Causes* ask about the past; *uses* ask about the future. What can I learn from this? Can I see this pain as splinters from His cross? Can I trust Him to use even bad for good, to bring good out of bad?

Yes, you can. You can say yes to His slow, mysterious plan of deliverance from evil, and you can believe it is wiser than our instant, quick-fix solutions.

Trust is an essential lesson we have to learn, and we can't learn to trust in the light but only in the dark. So He has to bring the dark.

So although we can't understand the reason for these bad things happening to these good people, we *can* understand why it has to be that way, we can understand why we can't understand.

Jesus did not suffer to take away our sufferings but to take away our sins. He did not suffer to take away our sufferings but to make them part of His. He did not suffer to take away our sufferings but to transform them. They are now doors to Heaven.

Death is the big door and pains are the little doors. He calls to us from behind them: I am here, behind this door, even though you can't see me, just as I am here behind the appearances of bread and wine in the Eucharist. Trust me. Take my hand and come. My hand has more nail marks in it than yours ever will. I am the master of pain, and I alone can lead you through the valley of the shadow of death. Fear no evil, for I am with you.

161. When I Die

If you love me, you will weep when I die. But weep not for me but for yourselves and your children.

Your tears may be tears of anger for a while, as well as tears of sadness, and if they are, they will probably be directed at God. Who else can you get angry at for death?

God is a target deep enough to take all the barbs and arrows of your anger and have them disappear into His body. The cross is bigger than the world.

But if you love me (and if you didn't, you wouldn't be angry), don't shoot. Don't shoot the arrows of your anger at God, even though you can't hurt Him. Because you can hurt yourself, and that would make me sad because I love you.

Let your tears come. "Not all tears are an evil," says Gandalf at the end of the greatest book of the 20th century. Let the love-tears come, but let them be love-tears only, not anger-tears. If you love me, then love God for creating me and giving me to you for a little while. Love Christ for saving me. Love your mother, my other half who is still with you. I am in her and she in me.

Swim in love always. Never dry up. Never stop surfing. I won't.

162. The Last Word

This is the last page of my little notebook. One day I will write the last page of the book of my life. You will too. That is life's only absolutely certain prediction. Yet we prepare for everything else with more care even though everything else is tiny compared with this. (The one unexpected feeling I had when I was present at my father's death was how *big* it was, how momentous, how heavy. It was bigger than anything I had experienced before, bigger than any event *in* life.)

No philosophy is worth your attention if it can't be professed on your deathbed.

No philosophy is as important as a person.

And there is only one person who has the answer to death. You know His name. May His name be your last word, as it shall be mine.

And then we will meet again, in the land of beginnings, not endings. And that will be a merry meeting!

All my love,
Your Dad

About the Author

Peter Kreeft is professor of philosophy at Boston College. He is the author of over fifty-five books, including *You Can Understand the Bible*, *Handbook of Christian Apologetics*, *The Philosophy of Tolkien*, and *The Sea Within*. He enjoys spending time with his four grown children and four grandchildren and lives in West Newton, Massachusetts, with his wife Maria.